FREELANCE WRITING FOR NEWSPAPERS

To Jim

FREELANCE WRITING FOR NEWSPAPERS

Jill Dick

A & C Black · London

First published 1991
A & C Black (Publishers) Limited
35 Bedford Row, London WC1R 4JH

© 1991 Jill Dick

ISBN 0-7136-3427-8

A CIP catalogue record for this book
is available from the British Library.

Typeset by ABM Typographics Ltd, Hull
Printed in Great Britain by Whitstable Litho Ltd.,
Whitstable, Kent

Contents

Standfirst

We Britons love reading newspapers more than eating, gardening or walking the dog. On an average day two out of three adults read a morning paper and every Sunday three-quarters of us relax with our weekend favourites. All those papers, plus all the evening, weeklies and freesheets are only read because someone has written what readers want to read.

Thousands of those writers are freelance journalists. That means they are not on the payroll of any paper; they just take it upon themselves to submit what they write to an editor, hoping he will like it sufficiently to print it and pay the writer for providing it. Freelances don't work in newspaper offices, in fact many never go near them, although later, when they become established, editors may start asking *them* for written work, in a reversal of the pattern of their early days.

Anyone can be a freelance, so what sort of writer will make a success of it? It will help if you have a real interest in local affairs and the wider national and international scene, and if you can write (or learn to write) lucidly, saying what you mean to say and making it easy to understand. Clumsy writing only holds up the flow of the text; that is why, for example, I eschew the tiresome custom of writing 'he or she, 'him or her' and so on in these pages, and leave readers to supply alternatives where appropriate, in whichever gender they prefer.

Appreciating the value of local paid-for and free papers in the community is also important but the characteristic without which freelancing could be an uphill struggle is a lively and instinctive (but not invasive) curiosity about people and events. That means at all times keeping your ears, eyes and – above all – your *mind* open.

Dedication to the task is essential. You may get a few ideas today, research into them a little next week and write your piece a month later, and even that unhurried approach will require a degree of discipline if your work is to be publishable.

Tighten up the whole schedule, determining that by a particular date or within a prearranged time you will think, study, research, write, rewrite and rewrite again – however many times it takes before you are satisfied – and a firm plan of action becomes necessary. How many hours a day or week will you give to freelancing? Will you devote set times to the separate activities required? Or do you only wish to write a little now and again when you have nothing else to do? There is no 'right' way and no 'wrong' way. In considering the quantity of writing, whatever you want is right for you. The quality of what you write, and that alone, will determine how successful you will be.

Working on their own, getting ideas, finding any facts they need, and choosing where to send what they've written is the way freelances prefer to write. Some writers whose names are household words work like this, but however practised at the job they might be now, at one time they knew nothing about it. Perhaps you don't know much about it yet; but where is the mighty oak that didn't start as a little acorn?

The advantages of freelancing are many. There is no daily grind of getting to and from an office, nobody restricts your work (yes, staff writers are bound to their employers and are not expected to write for other papers) and you can work when, where and how you wish, writing whatever you want for whichever papers you like without anyone looking over your shoulder and telling you what to do. You count that last point as a disadvantage, thinking you'd feel more confident if somebody *were* looking over your shoulder, at least at the beginning? That's understandable, although there is no mystique about freelance writing for newspapers.

For those who want to but don't know where or how to begin, this book is the answer. It cuts through what often appears a jungle where newcomers can't see the wood for the trees. I believe the horse comes before the cart (cliches are covered, too) so these pages provide a detailed guide to what papers exist before what-to-write or how-to-write-it. You will find techniques and working tips that journalists pick up over a lifetime in the job. Learn about paper density (no, not its thickness), intros, the shape of news, linkage, wimp words, come-ons, cut-offs and many other tricks of the trade.

Your status as a freelance is fully explored, with vital information about income tax, keeping records (and not just for tidiness or convenience), rights to keep and sell, libel and much more. Details of relevant reference books are supplied, with names and addresses of societies, organisations and individuals always ready to help.

How to make 'Letters to the Editor' work for you, facts and figures about what you should be paid, when, and what to do if you're not – it's all here, while a section showing how to prepare for a newspaper interview precedes taking the interview itself and the technique of writing it up later.

There is an intriguing insight into how newspapers are put together with modern direct input and on-screen layout as well as a revealing list of who-owns-what in this country's huge range of national and regional papers, locals and freesheets.

Finally comes an important chapter on what to do afterwards. When you've got your foot on the ladder, when every opportunity you take enriches your experience and stretches your talents – how do you, how do professionals, behave?

Newspapers are written and put together by people who have taken the time to learn how to do it and the trouble to practise and develop what they've learned. The reader may like to imagine it's all tossed off without anyone having to work very hard and that after your first day you'll be wearing a green eye shield and shouting 'Hold the front page!' The truth is that, with few exceptions, the finished product is due to craftsmanship unobserved by readers. We are in the middle of a revolution in the way papers are prepared and printed but the road to success remains as it was in the days of some of the 'greats' of Fleet Street. Almost sixty years ago Arthur Christiansen, editor of the *Daily Express* at only 29, recalled hours spent studying the London evening papers, line by line, column by column, contrasting headlines, news value, human interest and all the other ingredients of a newspaper. He learned, as thousands of people who write for newspapers have learned since, that it is always the ordinary people behind a story that make it live. People, to a journalist, are the breath of life.

'You've got blue blood,' an editor once growled at me when I tried to make him change his mind about the layout of a page in his newspaper. 'It's printing ink. Messy stuff and incurable.'

Well, I don't know about the mess; in these high-tech days the newspaper game is quite a clean business. But incurable – oh yes. And once you've got it, you may find you don't even want to be cured.

1
The Making of a Newspaper

The recent revolution

'Nobody will read newspapers now television can bring the very latest news right into our homes.' 'It's the death knell for newspapers.' We all heard such predictions a few years ago yet they're still very much alive, if not always quite as well as they'd like to be.

For practical proof consider the vast amount of paper used as newsprint, an amount that has varied little over the past 70 years. If you made a roll 30 inches wide and wound it round the earth *thirty-three thousand* times you might just have enough to supply all the newspapers printed in the United Kingdom in a single year. Newspapers are dying out?

They bounce back regardless of the competition of radio, television and even newscasts beamed to us from space, and while their function has altered subtly over the years, the changes in the way they're put together have proceeded at the gallop, accelerating in the past two or three years.

New systems of communication are being developed and improved with dramatic changes in equipment and working practices. Speed is everything, for a newspaper's life is short – at the most a fortnight, sometimes a week, in many cases only a day and often just a few hours. Failing to meet production deadlines is dire, and the penalty for delay may be not only a day's work lost but also another little nail being polished to hold down the lid of the coffin.

So the key words in the newspaper industry are (as they always have been) discipline, speed and accuracy. Anyone who has shared the smoke-hazed laid-back atmosphere of an editorial floor may have wondered how anything at all is going to be produced on time. It always is, somehow, and now it's achieved by something our fathers and grandfathers could hardly have dreamed of – computer technology. Copy (material for use) is not written in the office by typing words on paper, for there isn't any at this stage, but by 'direct input' (sometimes called 'direct entry'). This means computer keyboards resembling typewriter keys throw up the typed words onto screens rather like small television sets in front of the journalists. They can then delete errors, insert sentences, move whole paragraphs or import them from elsewhere, and perform many other wonderful manoeuvres, all at the touch of the correct keys. Anyone familiar with a word-processor will have first-hand experience of the same system on a personal level.

Of course the written editorial material is only a part of the whole newspaper; most of it will have already been written by journalists on the staff a day or more before it is wanted and work accepted from freelances outside the office will have been made ready for use. Many more people are also working busily in different ways for each individual issue well before the day of publication, which is itself such a regular event it seems almost commonplace. But the more you get to know about just how a newspaper gets put together the more of a marvel it is revealed to be. And when it's done and the paper is ultimately printed, it all has to be done again, perhaps the very next day. A miracle of expertise, enterprise and – now – technology awaits readers for just a few pence.

The first tasks in the preparation of a daily newspaper involve a lot of preplanning. Sales folk on the telephone and out around the area will have sold space for display and classified advertisements, and the spaces for them will have been allocated, as they always go in first. A leader writer will have had talks with the editor (who may choose to write it himself) and decisions will have been made about the topic of the lead, its width and length. Regular pieces like TV listings, the weather forecast and the crossword puzzle, for instance, will have been given their places. What is called 'soft' news (because it may be used more or less any time) and features, women's pages, specialists' columns and so on will have been placed, and the only spaces left are reserved for the 'hard' news that will surely come in all day long.

The whole process will be less tight on a weekly paper, but the principle will be the same and it will be put together in much the same order of priority. Freelance feature writers might be a little disappointed at the apparent lack of importance attached to the prose they've toiled over, but never fear that your work is not important because nobody's dashing around with it at the last minute. In fact if it gets a 'good' place on the page (that's traditionally a little right of centre on the top half of a right hand page, a spot to which, experts tell us, the eye is most naturally drawn) you can be reasonably confident it was considered important enough to hold that place. That doesn't mean, of course, that other spots in the paper are not important, but given the time and opportunity afforded by computer usage for easier movement of whole stories from one place to another on the page layout screen, more pages are now designed to please the eye than to satisfy editorial demands.

The practice developed a long time ago (and obtains on some papers to this day) that a story anywhere on the front page 'above the line', i.e. above the half way fold where the bottom half of the paper might not be visible in a newsagent's rack or on his counter, presented such a great sales factor that it should attract a higher rate of pay than the same story would in a less valued position. The truth is that every story in the paper is valuable for that day's issue, or it wouldn't be there. A paper that persistently prints little pieces by the editor's grandmother purely because she is his grandmother or takes a poorly-written story pushing an advertised product in place of a well-written one by a stranger – that paper soon goes out of business. Everything in this cut-throat world of competition, but *everything* is costed most carefully and each story, each picture, each word must earn its place.

As for the 'hard' news, that comes in all the time. It's not all the stuff that will make readers gasp, nor even mildly surprising, for in this 'hard' news category must come 'news' that is already expected. A local paper might be waiting for a statement from a regional fire chief, for instance, following a serious fire in a hospital or school; a regional evening would hope to catch the verdict from a particular trial; and a paper would soon lose favour with readers if it did not bother to get the result of a big football match or a report of a major race meeting. Much of the 'news' is not unexpected, but it is not actually to hand at the early layout stage.

One way and another, through avenues well-established and just occasionally by unexpected routes, the news comes in and eventually takes its place in the day's layout. Many highly skilled people handle the whole operation before it's time to 'put the paper to bed', and some of the work they do is described below. Eventually all is ready and another new technological marvel takes over. 'Facsimile transmission' allows all the editorial and advertising preparation to be done in one place and the actual printing to be done elsewhere, perhaps in several widely separated print units in other parts of the UK. It takes no longer and is equally easy to print the paper in a different country; the *Financial Times* prints its European edition in Frankfurt, while the *International Guardian* prints in Marseilles.

There is already plenty to marvel at with today's 'electronic' newspapers, and the experts tell us it's all only just beginning; desk top publishing at professional and commercial level is already poking its fascinating nose round the corner.

All national papers now enjoy the benefits of the technological revolution, but it was the provincial press that led the way, in some places being the first to use facsimile transmission back in the 1960s. Newspaper readers in Nottingham have a special reason to be proud.

Nottingham's historic 'first'

Until the mid-1980s workers in the newspaper industry had taken a resolute stand against any sort of modernisation. Equipment was outdated; old-fashioned working practices were the norm; union members were totally resistant to change. The 'closed shop' ruled, whereby only union members could be employed, and then only in rigorously defined categories. Almost a quarter of the total overhead costs went on the production side alone where wages were very high. Working on antiquated machines then in use nowhere else, men in the print machine rooms, for instance, could earn more than £700 a week. Small wonder they clung to their jobs so tenaciously.

The National Graphical Association and the National Union of Journalists, with a few other smaller associated unions, had a tight monopoly on all the labour without which a newspaper cannot function. They knew that if the new technology were allowed to take over manpower levels would be greatly reduced and many of them would be out of work. But at the start of the 1980s new Employment Acts banned picketing and closed shops – and Fleet Street was never the same again.

Eddie Shah was the first major publisher to test the new legislation and employ non-union labour at his Warrington plant, previously used to print his successful range of freesheets. A lengthy and ugly dispute ended in bitter wrangling, and the NGA was fined more than £625,000 for contempt and for damaging his business. It was not until the following year, 1984, that the real breakthrough came.

The credit for taking advantage of the changes in the law went to the *Nottingham Evening Post*. NGA and NUJ members were outnumbered and the paper made history by being the first newspaper to introduce direct input, enabling journalists to write their stories straight onto screens, edit them, and send them on their way to the next production stage. Thanks to the new technology, fewer than 30 composers were able to do the work previously done by well over 200, allowing production time and financial saving for more pages to be added to the paper. It was a great step forward for the Nottingham paper; for the rest of the newspaper world it was an eye-opener as to what could be done and what soon would be done.

Provincials ahead

So it was that the provincials got the bit between their teeth while the nationals were still battling with their obsolete equipment and outdated working methods. The indefatigable Eddie Shah, encouraged by his victory in principle if not in practice, pressed forward with an even more ambitious plan. He launched a new daily to be titled *Today*. In the changed climate the circumstances were more propitious, but there were enormous difficulties to be overcome. The technology was hugely expensive and quite new to everyone on the paper; breakdowns were frequent and costly; deadlines were often late or missed altogether. It was a gallant but hopeless struggle and eventually the paper was lost to Rupert Murdoch's News UK empire for production at his new Wapping site. That in itself was a front-page story for many weeks with some of the ugliest scenes occurring in recent years witnessed on television sets all over the world. Whatever it did to industrial relations in the newspaper world, it proved to be a major breakthrough in publishing history. Within two or three years every major newspaper in the UK had followed Murdoch out of Fleet Street, and all had adopted the new technology.

While this was happening to the big boys their country cousins in the provinces were moving over to a totally new way of working with hardly any fuss. It is of great value to freelance writers that even small-town papers are now using direct input. Is your local paper doing so? Remember that the technological revolution is not confined to the paper's office, nor are its advantages limited to professional writers on the regular staff. Some freelance writers are finding they can write their copy at home, on their own word-processors, and then hand their floppy disks over to their paper. Others possess the right equipment (which is neither exorbitantly costly nor incomprehensible) and can transmit copy straight to the newspaper office to which they might otherwise have posted or hand-delivered it. The right equipment could consist of a modem, a device for enabling you to transmit what is written on your floppy disk at home by telephone lines to the newspaper, without the use of any paper or the need to speak into the phone. Or, if you feel happier actually seeing your copy written down and again if you have the right equipment, you could place a sheet of your copy onto a 'fax' (short for 'facsimile') machine and the paper's office would almost instantly find the plain paper they had put in their 'fax' machine covered by your words, for 'fax' is just a different method of transmitting what you have written directly onto a piece of paper at their end. Clever, eh?

All this high-technology is invaluable for the freelance so don't imagine it is way above your head and that it doesn't matter if you can't understand it. There was quite an outcry at the difficulty of managing electric typewriters some years ago, and who could then have imagined an inexpensive home computer, for instance, being available for every home? The equipment needed above is not wildly expensive (well, are you in the newspaper business or aren't you?) and the price of all electronic gadgetry is coming down fast. Before you splash out you should establish that the papers you most frequently wish to contribute to do have the capacity to receive your copy electronically (an increasing number now do) and that whatever hardware you buy is compatible with theirs. You then need to inform the paper that you will be filing copy this way and ask for their specific instructions. Whatever they say, it won't be difficult to follow.

Of course submitting work to the newspaper's office in the traditional way is still perfectly acceptable to offices equipped with modern technology, but it is exciting to contemplate what the future may have in store for freelance writers. Perhaps a few years hence we'll wonder how we ever managed to get stories written and copy to the paper by that old-hat way of writing it on paper, making a black, putting the copy in an envelope, finding a stamp, going round to the pillar box....

The staff and what they do

On a major national daily it is normal for each separate job in the making of a newspaper to be done by a particular individual who does nothing else. But a small local weekly or a low-circulation freesheet may number the staff on the fingers of one hand. I once worked for a couple of months on a weekly which appeared to have been struck by the plague, for only the elderly editor, a boy messenger with spots and a yearning to be more important, and I remained. For outside assistance we had one generally inebriated photographer straight out of *The Importance of Being Earnest* and a 15-mile distant printing plant on which we were relieved to deposit everything each Tuesday morning. It was an experience that greatly broadened my idea of who-does-what on a newspaper, as the editor and I did the lot, often working all hours until the paper was put to bed.

I never heard whether the messenger boy climbed the ladder to success. If he did and is now, in 1990, on the staff of a weekly paper outside London he is probably working with some 14 other journalists, four of them trainees, will have a better than even chance of working on new technology and will be earning an average £166 per week as a reporter or £198 as a sub-editor. On an evening paper he'll be doing better as one of about 68 on the staff; he will have a 55% chance of working on new technology and earn, on average, a weekly £223 as a reporter or £258 as a sub-editor. Nationals, of course, have larger staffs; for instance, *The Guardian* has 250. For all I know that messenger boy may now be the editor of one of our leading weekly papers. If he is, he will have learned the hard way with a taste of at least some of the jobs referred to below.

Newspapers are generally organised into _five_ main departments, but this varies greatly according to their size. In any case the use of computer technology is leading to more and more independence in departments; on major papers classified advertising, for instance, is now often so huge an operation that it may demand separate management and its own typesetting department.

The five main departments are 1) editorial – which will be the main concern of the readers of this book; 2) administration – the building, secretarial, finance, stationery etc.; 3) production – composing and printing, including paper, machinery, pictures etc.; 4) sales, and 5) advertising. All these cost money but only the last two bring the paper any income. In fact on some papers even department 4) runs at a net loss, having enormous expenses in itself. What a weight of responsibility rests on the people in the advertising department!

Back to the editorial side, and generally the first hurdle for 'outside' copy to jump is the copytaster. He will be a skilled and experienced journalist who will estimate the relative value of news stories and how many will be needed for the editorial space known to be available. As the job title indicates, the copytaster decides to accept or reject unsolicited copy. There may be a conversation with the editor before a decision is reached, or (on a smaller paper) the editor may himself be the copytaster. Work already commissioned by the head of a particular department, such as the features editor, will not be subject to a further decision at this stage.

The editor of a national paper is like a commander in chief. In this lies one of the major differences between a newspaper and a magazine: a newspaper is nearly always a complete editorial, advertising and production operation all in one, whereas a magazine will normally subcontract the production side out to some other organisation. The editor of a newspaper, therefore, will be the overseer of all departments and is responsible for the whole editorial content as well as for the style and image of the paper. How much he chooses to work at the daily or weekly job himself is often a matter of personal choice; some prefer to spend their time in meetings, leaving the staff to run the day-to-day business; others can't stay away from the scene of action, perhaps preferring to write their own leader columns and be involved with the running of all departments. On smaller papers where staff numbers are lower, the editor won't be able to sit in policy-making solitude for long, and may happily spend days as busily as any of the staff, turning a hand to any job in the office that needs doing. So it's a man-of-all-work editor for the small papers, an editor-in-chief with deputies and assistants for the big ones and almost certainly a mixture of both between the two. Only a personal acquaintance with your local paper will let you into the secret of who actually does what and you may have a surprise when you find out.

The main sections in the editorial department on a national paper cover home news, foreign news, features, pictures and sport although the last is sometimes considered a separate department on its own. Each section boasts its own editor (and maybe even assistants) as well as staff writers and reporters attached for varying periods to each. The news editors look after all incoming news, with the foreign editor responsible for selecting and working on all stories coming in from overseas and the work of foreign correspondents (see below). In addition to this are the political and parliamentary correspondents and the financial and industrial staff. Somewhere bridging the hard and soft news come the diarists who may be live (like Lady Olga Maitland) or imaginary (like William Hickey). Feature writers and the sports department produce a predetermined proportion of the paper's copy, while the pictures or 'pix' are the preserve of another important section.

Pix apart, all the above are concerned with doing the actual writing of the paper. So where might your submitted piece fit into this jigsaw? Firstly, if it's an accepted or commissioned feature it will be closely scrutinised by one or more of the sub-editors, those most important people, whose job is to make it and all the other staff-written and freelance copy ready to be printed.

It is the chief-subs and subs who exert the most impact on how the paper will look when it is finished, for their tasks include checking the facts, correcting grammar and punctuation to conform to the house style, writing crossheads and headlines with setting instructions (headlines sell papers, especially on Sundays, more than the contents or even what's on the rest of the front page) and giving the printers full information about the size, shape and typography of each story. Typography is a fascinating subject and the ability to select the right typeface and use it to best effect is a most valuable skill. Readers know their papers by the 'look' of the type and there is often an outcry when it changes. Does not 8 point Times Roman give the text of *The Times* a special authority (whether it deserves it or not)? It's 7 point Excelsior for the *News of the World* text, Baskerville for *The Observer* headlines and Ionic for *Daily Mail* text. Type is measured in points, a point being 0.01383 of an inch, which gives approximately 72 points to the inch. But this refers to the depth of the body of metal on which a letter stands, not to the actual size of the letter. Owing to the bevels at the top and bottom of the little metal block, the actual face size is always less than the body size. To establish a working norm it is accepted in the printing world that the point size equals the total size of the lower case alphabet. This is measured from the top of the highest 'ascender' (d, for instance) to the bottom of the lowest 'descender' (like q).

Every writers' gathering hears complaints from irate freelances about the alteration or ruin of their copy by a sub-editor on some paper or magazine at sometime. But the work of the subs is not easy. It will vary according to the size of a paper and its frequency of publication, but consider how you would interpret the job specification: to shape the material in the form of presentation decided by the chief sub so as to bring out the point of a story, to condense it more effectively than can be done by cutting, and to make it more readable. A sub must also have a sound knowledge of the laws of libel and contempt, of central and local government organisation, of the various types of court and the pitfalls to be avoided when reporting from them, of newspaper terms, of the organisation for which he works and the paper's edition times, with deadlines of copy, pix and pages. (*The Guardian*, for example, prints four editions: at 9.15 pm, 10.30 pm, 12.15 pm, and 1.30 am.)

Added to this a sub-editor must ensure the copy is in good taste and good English, while observing the writer's own concept and the needs of the reader. It must also be the required length and shape. Quite an exacting job, isn't it? And that's only looking at it from the freelance writer's point of view. Subs also cope with copy from reporters, news agencies, public relations and publicity sources, prepare the text for the printers with all the acknowledged methods of marking, advise layout subs about lengths of stories and page layouts, perhaps write revised stories to include later material on those already running, handle pictures, maybe act as copytaster as well, selecting stories for special importance, human interest, entertainment value...and through it all they must keep calm and practical. If you want a quiet life on a newspaper, don't aim to be a sub-editor!

Because a great deal of a paper's success depends on how it looks, sales being in relation to appearance rather than news content, the best tabloid headline and layout subs are highly paid. As well as the duties listed above they must be ready to deal with copy arriving often in quantity and certainly with increasing speed and urgency as the paper's deadline approaches. Life on the sub's table of a major regional evening paper on Budget Day, with a Chancellor of the Exchequer agonisingly slow to reveal the nitty-gritty everyone wants to know, is not an experience for the faint-hearted. (I am

surprised to have lived through such gruelling days myself.)
Eventually page layouts are prepared so the compositors
have an exact guide to the appearance of each page when it's
made up. Whole books have been written about the changes
in the printing of newspapers. For the freelance writer it is
enough to know that all the editorial matter, completed as
above, goes with the advertising material (and the pix, from
their own department) to the page compositors, is made into
plates and is – at last – printed. This absorbing process is now
at the front of the technological revolution with
'phototypesetting' and offset lithography, more commonly
known as 'web-offset', bringing a basically new meaning to
newspaper production. Better quality, greater flexibility,
more pages and potentially increased readership are just
some of the prizes that lie ahead for those that survive. And
the more that do, the more opportunities there are for the
freelance writer.

Finally comes the 'ombudsman'. Yes, all the major papers
now have their own ombudsmen whose job is to cope with
complaints from the public. As you may guess, ombudsmen
are people of considerable experience in journalism and – like
ombudsmen in other fields – they need enormous reserves of
patience and understanding. These appointments are part of
a new Code of Conduct signed by almost all national papers,
but the establishment of ombudsmen isn't without its critics
as they are appointed by editors. Is not the essence of
impartiality that there should be no such conflict of interest?
Time will tell.

Outside specialists

It pays to remember that the larger a newspaper the more it
can afford to pay specialists to write on particular topics.
These writers will often be freelances themselves who by dint
of impressing the editor or features editor with their expertise
and *ability to write about it* have gained a 'standby' place among
the paper's contacts. Study of your own paper might reveal a
regular antiques column, a weekly cookery corner or that the
same columnist is on hand with an authoritative view on
aircraft construction, for example, at the time of any major air
disaster. Wise beginners will naturally avoid these topics, and
spot ones that do not feature regularly. Leading papers will
also employ regular and occasional overseas correspondents.
They will be based in key cities round the world, such as Hong

Kong, Moscow or Washington, and they will always be prepared to fly to 'flash points' within their reach when required.

Back home other correspondents cover a variety of topics ranging from music and live theatre to Stock Exchange fluctuations and clay-pigeon shooting. Political and parliamentary correspondents are highly skilled and experienced writers who are rarely seen as they spend most of their time at Westminster. Their job is to report on parliamentary debates and affairs and to write notes and sketches. Meanwhile Lobby corespondents are busy sounding out what's going on behind the scenes, writing background reports and trying to interpret Government actions and ideas. Don't pine to be a Lobby correspondent, because – officially – they· don't exist! This sounds such a paradox I've always held them in special affection, and actually met a couple one misty evening in Parliament Square when falling snow was deadening sound; real cloak-and-dagger stuff. They receive information provided by Government spokesmen, but you'd never get them to admit what was going on, for it's usually off the record. Every time you read 'It is understood from Government sources...' or 'Rumours in Whitehall suggest...' you'll know they're there.

News-gathering

If newspapers are about anything they should logically be about news and it is this part of putting the paper together that is the most lively. A major paper will have news flooding in all day, coming from many different sources. Teams of reporters (often each section of the paper has its own team) will be out and about gathering news, phoning it in, ringing for photographers, asking for further instructions and keeping the subs table busy. So if a 'good' news story breaks just where you happen to be the paper won't care that you're not a regular member of the staff; they'll want to know about it. (See Chapter 3, 'What to Write'.) On the home news front local and smaller papers serving a defined circulation area get their up-to-date news of what's happening by doing the 'calls' – just asking around. Other news stories will originate from readers phoning in with tip-offs about interesting pieces of news that might be worth following up. Press releases about forthcoming events already in the pipeline and about 'new' matters pour into newspaper offices, and some will carry the germ of a newsworthy story; off will go a reporter to investigate. But for the big papers, at least, the most valuable providers of news are the established press agencies, who are in business for nothing else.

News agencies

Almost all newspapers rely on news coming on the 'wire' from one or more of the four big news agencies: Reuters, which is British, Agence Presse France, and the American Associated Press and United Press International. Provincial papers may depend on the Press Association, this country's national agency.

Newspapers subscribe to one or more of the above and perhaps to some of the smaller agencies which have been set up in many other countries to gather news from all over the world and transmit it quickly and reliably to anyone who wants it. Modern technology has had a profound effect on the methods of distributing news; it is estimated that some 5 million words per day are received by various newspapers in London on the wire, though of course only a proportion of them are actually used.

Features

More freelance feature material comes into the average newspaper than any other sort of freelance copy. Indeed, when most freelance writers think of writing for newspapers they automatically think of features, and nothing else. As the chapter titled 'What to Write' indicates, freelance submissions are often needed for many other sections of the paper. But if it's going to be a feature, the first essential is to study published features carefully in your chosen market.

The space to be allocated to feature material is carefully determined according to the paper's size, and the amount of space given over to advertisements and news. The former brings in revenue, the latter has to be paid for. Features also cost money (not enough, in the opinion of many freelances) but they are exclusive and valuable to the paper. Establish yourself as a reliable and authoritative feature writer on a newspaper and you may become one of the little band the editor knows he can call on when required.

Sharp practice

One might imagine life is cushy for newspaper editors. Plenty of news comes in, advertising space is sold and there's a steady thump of unsolicited features hitting the desk with the morning mail. In truth it isn't always like that. Well-organised papers have a junior entering in a book the titles of all copy that arrives each day, regardless of its eventual fate. Not so our easy-going editor who doesn't want too much hassle. Sometimes, perhaps, there are so many new features arriving that they don't all get read. Maybe one of those stuck in a heap getting dustier as the days go by is yours. The cleaning lady has a purge. Unread copy gets pushed aside and lost. As weeks have passed since you posted your feature off and you've heard nothing about it, you query. It can't be found and nobody has any knowledge of it ever having arrived because nobody made a note of it anywhere. That's just one bad habit, and there are others more sinister.

The editor of a small weekly might realise copy's a bit short as some of the staff are on holiday and a couple are off sick; bound to be enough good stuff in the post, surely? Maybe there is, and perhaps you wrote it. Alas, not all freelance material carries the correct byline when it appears in print. An unscrupulous sub-editor can alter a paragraph here, move a couple of sentences there and rewrite some of the most distinctive phrases in other places. 'It's mine!' you protest! You'll quickly discover that nothing is as dead as yesterday's copy, and by the time your protest has been listened to a fortnight or so has elapsed. Oh dear.

Nor is this 'lifting' as it's euphemistically called ('stealing' is the word I prefer) confined to little provincial papers where the lifters hope nobody's going to notice. Weeklies who don't mind lifting from other sources know that the stories they're likely to be covering are also likely to be featured in the regional dailies or evening papers also covering their areas; work that has been researched and written up by those who have already published is sometimes at risk. Lazy editors find using the bones of someone else's story (sometimes with the flesh still attached) is much less work than getting it for themselves.

The popular dailies are big offenders and they're not fussy where they lift from: at the time of writing a High Court ruling is making Express Newspapers and *Today* pay each other damages for lifting from each other and the *Daily Mirror* is suing *The Sun*. Stories in overseas publications, sent in from news agencies or mentioned on radio and television are rich 'source' material just waiting to be given a new byline. Almost any name will do and the writer credited with having written the story may not even be a real person; use a phantom reporter, goes the twisted logic, and you won't be getting a real one into trouble if there is any.

Reuters complain bitterly that most national papers are guilty, with even the apparently respectable *Financial Times* crediting Reuters material to 'our Financial Staff'. A feature writer who had a story he had written appear in the London *Evening Standard* under the byline of a *Standard* journalist said it was like having caterers round to cook your meal and then telling the guests you've done it yourself. Whatever you call it or whatever it's like, it leaves a nasty taste in the mouth.

Baddies exist in every field, and I hasten to assure you they are vastly outnumbered by honest folk. It's just a pity the sourness they cause can bring individual newspapers and the whole industry into disrepute.

Jargon

Most occupations have their own jargon, much of it originating long ago and referring to working practices now out of date. It is not surprising that by the very nature of their business those whose work is words enjoy a particularly rich store of jargon. Here is some of it:

agency copy	material coming from a major news agency
ampersand	'&', the typographical sign for 'and'
banner	the main headline across the top of the page
body type	the size of type used for most of the paper
black	a duplicate, photocopy or carbon copy
bold	thick dark type used for emphasis
byline	a writer's name at the head of a story
caps	capital letters
caption	explanatory text below or beside a pic
cast-off	ending a story, generally in a given space
catchline	an identifying phrase/word at the top of a page
copy	any matter to be set in type
crosshead	a sub-heading, often in bold type, to enliven text
deadline	the time by which a story must be filed
draft	a temporary or unfinished story

ear	the advertising space beside front page title-line
edition	a one-time print (perhaps with regional variations)
embargo	the time for publication of a pre-released story
file	to submit copy for publication
freebie	a gift or privilege from a reader/advertiser
fudge box	space for late news. Also an item in a ruled box
house style	spelling, punctuation etc. as the paper likes it
intro	the opening paragraph
layout	sheet ruled into columns showing where copy will go
lead	the main news story in the paper
lift	to pass off someone else's work as your own
literal	a printing error in spelling ect (*sic*)
lower case	small (not capital) letters
masthead	heading on editorial page giving details of paper
NIBS	small items of news, News In Brief pars
par	a paragraph
point	a standard unit of type size. Also a full-stop
proofs	the first print for checking before the final print
run on	where a story is not to be broken into pars
slush	a pile of unsolicited and often unwanted copy
spike	an imaginary or actual spike for rejected copy
standfirst	an intro separate from the story itself
story	a written item or piece of work
streamer	a page lead printed across several columns
stringer	writer (usually overseas) always ready to file copy
splash	a page one lead story
strap	a subsidiary headline above a main headline
shorts	small stories for fillers or down-page items
tag	the small type line after the main headline
tabloid	a page half the size of a broadsheet
tear-sheet	a page carrying published copy
upper case	capital letters
widow	a word alone on a line

2
Markets

National papers

In Britain there are 12 daily papers and 10 Sunday papers, and all, like provincial and local papers, in private ownership. That means there is no direct government control or restraint, and virtually all papers are financially independent from any political masters. Per head of population we read more newspapers than any other country in the world. How we manage to do so is partly luck, in that we are small enough to allow all our national newspapers to be distributed around Britain on a single day. But also, more importantly, we have a great assortment of newspapers in healthy competition with each other, and that ensures there is something to satisfy everyone. The provincial press vastly overshadows the nationals, local papers are rooted in the population's affections and the number of new freesheets continues to increase. There's never any shortage of newspapers to read – or to write for. Take a broad look at their attitudes and aims – if you could, with so many thousands to consider – and you would find them almost as varied as the people who read them. News, background stories and interesting items may be their staple fare, but there is a fascinating extra dimension about newspapers. They are not just inky words and pictures printed on greyish-white paper; in a sense all their own, newspapers are *alive*.

In their pages you can expect to read about the events of the day, covering anything and everything, from changes at a local factory and a fire in a city library to the illness of an international footballer, the financial crisis of an orchestra and the latest gyrations of international personalities; all is grist to the mill. Writers, appreciating that not all appears immediately before the eyes, know that only a careful study of the newspapers will reveal their instinctive social and/or political slant, and particular views in general or on a current topic. This is the market study between the lines, one might say, and just as one meeting with a new acquaintance will not reveal his whole character, so newspapers need to be studied thoroughly, with an awareness of what-to-look-for over a period of time, if they are to be understood. A local weekly paper is a good starting point and for many people this will be where the early successes are scored. Never belittle your own work when you sell to these markets and to 'free' papers; the word 'provincial' has no place here wearing its condescending hat. Weeklies are as important a part of the whole business as any of their mass-circulation daily and regional cousins. Local papers usually stay around longer too, and the contributor whose work can survive repeated study by what is often a personally-involved and intensely critical readership is doing very well indeed.

It is important to aim high in your writing. In the newspaper world that means achieving and maintaining a high standard in all the work you do, wherever you may be submitting it and regardless of where it is published. Quality writing is as much 'quality' in a local weekly or a free paper as in a national or regional daily; aim 'high' in all you write and you can hardly fail.

'I could never write for a national paper!' you may be protesting. But a good deal of their daily contents is written by ordinary men and women, some of whom didn't even think of themselves as writers until they saw their first submissions in print. They write to the papers simply because they have something to say: to let others share their griefs, or their laughs, or something that has made a good or bad impact on their lives. They hope other ordinary people, viz. readers, will be interested – and they are. One young man wrote a blow-by-blow account for the *News of the World* of how he came to love the once-loathed mother-in-law he lived with, and judging by the enormous response from readers his initially sad, finally heart-warming and very funny story touched many hearts. (When you remember that in this country one person in three over fifteen years old reads the *News of the World* that's a lot of hearts.) *The Guardian* published a middle-aged widow's reaction when unthinking comforters said, 'What a good thing you've got another,' after her elder daughter was killed in a road accident; a handicapped writer was thrilled to see her recipes printed in a leading daily, and writing for weekend colour supplements is no longer a novelty for a hard-working freelance who has learned how to be a thorough professional without going near a training school for journalists. You can never be certain what may be published or where. For a long time I feared Heaven would fall down if a day passed without something I'd written appearing in a national paper somewhere in the world. It's still up there, isn't it? (Honesty forces me to confess this exhausting obsession no longer haunts me, which is just as well for all of us down here on earth.)

So I begin a brief survey of markets (the topic would take this and several more booksful if I let it) with the national papers, not in deference to any mistaken idea of their superiority, but because I have to start somewhere. My admiration of the enthusiasm, pace and stamina that sustain them extends to the far wider sphere of the hard-working provincial press with something approaching awe.

National papers are referred to either as 'qualities' or as 'tabloids' (originally because of their paper size). The qualities are physically larger than the tabloids and are printed on paper of a size known as broadsheet. The term 'heavies' is seldom heard these days in describing the quality papers, although Sunday delivery boys might find the term appropriate when weighed down with the range of supplements and colour magazines that the weekend qualities now include. *The Sunday Times* alone weighs about two pounds.

Fifty-five per cent of all newspapers are home delivered; after all the big business and high technology that goes into them, the last vital task of getting them into the hands of readers is left to an army of schoolchildren working for pocket-money.

The qualities take a serious view of the news, supporting it with informed analysis and comment on political, economic, social and world events, news and comment being kept firmly apart. The arts, business, entertainment, sport, finance, women's affairs, employment and leisure pages feature in all; most of the material for these pages is provided by staff writers but there is always room for a good freelance who has done a properly-researched and well-written job. Motoring, opera, bridge, tapestry – are these your special subjects? They and many others have provided a first success for freelances who feared they'd never find a way in.

Leader pages may reveal a paper's editorial policy, while most have periods of giving particular attention to special groups of readers and what are judged to be their requirements: women (sometimes of a selected age and income group), sports enthusiasts, followers of a current political cause, and classes of readers chosen for topical or other reasons may be targeted by a newspaper for attention – and such deliberate policies will change from time to time. This is but one reason why we can support so many newspapers at once, and why careful study of them is essential for the would-be contributor. Nothing replaces personal market study for each potential writer may have something individual to contribute. In general terms the middle-range *Daily Mail* and *Daily Express* favour a wide coverage with features for women and the home, and general interest stories while *Today* is rather more dashing in its battle for young people (especially women) 'going places'. As the first daily newspaper to introduce colour in its pages, it often sees itself as being in the forefront of new thought and opinion, and its features tend to reflect this optimism.

Sunday qualities follow much the same style and most publish several sections and/or colour magazines, the notion being that at the weekends the nation has more time for seriously digesting the state of the world. Leisure takes prominence in Sunday supplements and in 1989 *The Daily Telegraph* and *The Independent* tried to catch the traditional Sunday leisure readers by bringing out their weekend magazines – as more of a mix of daily and weekend papers – on Saturdays. Competition is fierce; *The Guardian* and *The Times* responded by adding extra sections to their Saturday papers. Perhaps owing to the staff having more time to give to Sunday papers, they are traditionally harder for freelances to crack – harder but not impossible. Fillers for the *News of the World*, say, sharpen the mind, train the senses, are not hard to write and can lead on to bigger things.

The tabloid papers sell in far greater numbers than the others (12.2 million as against 2.7 million) with *The Sun* and the *Daily Mirror* taking the top two places in the league table. Their appeal relies on content and approach, the emphasis being on human interest and sensational stories (especially in the world of show biz), sport and unpretentious light-hearted family entertainment. Tabloid Sundays adopt the same pattern as their daily counterparts and the tabloids still have the last laugh over their heavier rivals with the *News of the World* selling more than 5 million copies, making it the largest selling Sunday newspaper in the Western world.

Scotland, Wales and Northern Ireland also enjoy a flourishing press. There are six morning, six evening and four

Sunday papers in Scotland, two of which – the *Scotsman* and the *Glasgow Herald* – enjoy a circulation extending far beyond Scotland's borders. *Scotland on Sunday* publishes in London as well as in Edinburgh and Glasgow.

Wales can boast only one daily morning newspaper, the *Western Mail*, circulating mainly in south Wales, and otherwise relies on the Liverpool-published *Daily Post* for coverage of Welsh affairs. But there are several home-based evening papers and in 1989 the *Western Mail* launched a Sunday version titled *Wales on Sunday*.

One Sunday and two morning papers are published in Belfast, while papers from Eire are also widely read in Northern Ireland.

Here is straight-from-the-editor's-mouth information about what the nationals look for from potential contributors. I am grateful to all the papers below who recently supplied me with details of their current requirements. The full address of each appears at the end of this chapter. All nationals have FREEFONE numbers mainly used for filing copy, but you may not always be able to discover them!

TABLOID DAILIES:

Daily Mirror
Editor: Roy Greenslade
Very little copy is bought unsolicited. In the features area fees are agreed on commission and method of delivery.

Daily Star
Editor: Brian Hitchin
Virtually no freelance opportunities.

The Sun
Editor: Kelvin Mackenzie
Likes gossip and sensation, especially about pop and TV stars, people in the public eye etc. Probably little chance for inexperienced feature writers.

More or less 'in the middle' are:

Daily Express
Editor: Nicholas Lloyd
Generally welcomes unsolicited copy. Approach the relevant department by letter first.

Daily Mail
Editor: Sir David English
Little scope for the inexperienced writer.

Today
Editor: David Montgomery
Features editor: Tessa Hilton
Commissioned articles only. Unsolicited articles rarely if ever used. Payment by agreement.

Of a separate vintage is the old *Daily Worker*, now called:

Morning Star
Editor: Tony Chater
Feature space very competitive.

QUALITY DAILIES:

Financial Times
Editor: Richard Lambert
Features editor: Andrew Gowers
Contact by phone first to features editor, Roland Adburgham (Home News editor) or Max Wilkinson (Weekend FT editor). 'We use little from outside contributors. Weekend FT is always keen, nonetheless, to consider interesting ideas; feature pages are virtually entirely written by staff. Payment around £200+ per 1,000 words, ranging up to double that depending on piece, position etc.'

The Daily Telegraph
Editor: Max Hastings
Features editor: Veronica Wadley
News editor: James Allan
Most helpful and obliging. Likes a query letter first to the features editor. Requirements can only be assessed by the freelance studying that section of the paper for which his work would be appropriate: style and length are vital. 'We receive a great number of items which are useless because they do not fit any particular "department". We mainly take· items from experienced, proven writers who are acknowledged in their specialities: e.g. health, cooking, industry, politics etc. We only accept hard news as "tips", except from accredited journalists known to us.' Payment by arrangement but always above NUJ rates.

The Guardian
Editor: Peter Preston
Features editor: Richard Gott
Of all the nationals this has the largest number of specialist pages using freelance material. Submit to the features editor in the first place but copy must be aimed at a specific section.

The Independent
Editor: Andreas Whittam Smith
Features editor: David Robson
Contact features editor by letter first. 'We take very little freelance news and all must be ordered. Copy must be electronically fed. Payment around £100 per thousand words.'

The Times
Editor: Simon Jenkins
Features editor: Brigid Callaghan
Query the features editor by letter before making a submission.

TABLOID SUNDAYS:

Sunday Express
Editor: Robin Morgan
Features editor: Max Davidson
Contact Max Davidson by phone first. 'General interest, showbusiness features no more than 1,000 words. Payment varies.'

Sunday Mirror
Editor: Eve Pollard
Features editor: Robert Wilson
Generally welcomes unsolicited copy and likes first contact to be made by letter.

Sunday Sport
Editor: Drew Robertson
Caters for a section of male 18–35 readership.

The Mail on Sunday
Editor: Stewart Steven

Features editor: Jonathan Margolis
Query the features editor first by letter or (preferably) by phone. Requirements: 'Brilliant, very concise, original news-based features; no requirement for long think pieces or "little me and my microwave" type articles. Absolutely no need for anything which has appeared in any form anywhere else. Payment well above NUJ rates and very high indeed for the right piece – ideas also very well rewarded. A very hard market to penetrate but very rewarding and exciting if you do.'

The News of the World
Editor: Patricia Chapman
Features editor: A. Harris
News editor: R. Warren
Contact News or Features Desk by phone first. Payment by arrangement.

The People
Editor: Richard Stott
Likes gossip about big names.

QUALITY SUNDAYS:

Sunday Telegraph
Editor: Trevor Grove
Features editor: Richard Addis
Query by letter first to Richard Addis/Features or James Langton/News. Pays NUJ rates.

The Independent on Sunday
Editor: Stephen Glover
Authoritative copy is written almost exclusively by staff journalists, but specialist writers may find an opening. Contact by letter first.

The Observer
Editor: Donald Trelford
Unsolicited contributions should be addressed to the Editor and they will be directed to the appropriate department. Payment by negotiation.

The Sunday Times
Editor: Andrew Neil
Query first by letter or phone to head of section concerned.
Payment by arrangement, above NUJ rates.

Published weekly on Fridays is:

The European
Editor: Ian Watson
The first weekly to attempt comprehensive coverage of European affairs, with sections covering news, politics, business, sport, culture and lifestyle. Study of the paper is essential before attempting to make contact.

Who owns what

Although several of the above papers are owned by partnerships of proprietors or by individuals, most are in the hands of limited liability companies. *The Independent* was launched in 1986 and is funded by journalists anxious to avoid what they fear as manipulation by a proprietor. The best known independent newspaper is *The Guardian* which is owned by the Scott Trust, set up in 1936 to maintain the journalistic and commercial principles of C.P. Scott, editor and proprietor of the then *Manchester Guardian* for 50 years. (The company now also has a 10% stake in the Spanish *El Mundo*.)

Not withstanding such individual enterprises, a handful of 'giants' now own and run the majority of Britain's national and provincial papers. As many of the giants' empires also include commercial involvement all over the world – in television, shipping, property, airlines, oil, insurance and high-level commerce, for example – tremendous power in the world of communications rests in their hands. Your weekly paper may seem just the local rag you view with some affection but wouldn't credit with much importance beyond its immediate circulation area: in reality it is probably a small cog in a very big business indeed.

Anxiety about too much power being controlled by the same proprietor surfaces every time there is a newspaper merger or one swallows up another, and so it should. It is illegal to 'transfer a newspaper or newspaper assets to a proprietor whose newspapers have an average daily circulation, with that of the newspaper to be taken over, of

500,000 or more copies, without the written consent of the Secretary of State for Industry' but the big moguls search to find loopholes in legal complexities. Sometimes they win, sometimes they lose.

Rupert Murdoch owns *The Sun*, the *News of the World*, *The Times*, *The Sunday Times*, *The Times Educational Supplement*, *The Times Literary Supplement*, the *Times Higher Educational Supplement* and *Today*. He also owns more than 20 American newspapers, a dozen in his native Australia, has large magazine holdings in many countries including Britain, owns publishers Collins and Harper & Row, 20th Century Fox, Sky Television and part of Reuters. Robert Maxwell owns the *Daily Mirror*, the *Sunday Mirror*, *The People*, the *Daily Record*, *Sunday Mail*, *The Sporting Life*, and the English language *China Daily*. He founded and owns Pergamon Press (who publish no fewer than 550 periodicals under various imprints), owns US publisher Macmillan, Britain's largest network of cable channels and has wide interests in broadcasting and television. His unique concept of a pan-European newspaper titled *The European* was launched in mid-May 1990 with printing in Hungary and West Germany as well as in this country, and editor Ian Watson hopes for a targeted circulation of 250,000 here with about 100,000 in Europe. Both these two press barons also bought stakes in Hungarian newspapers in their newly-found freedom at the end of the 1980s.

Conrad Black is the owner of *The Daily Telegraph*, the *Sunday Telegraph*, *The Spectator*, and some 50 other titles. David Robert Stevens (Lord Stevens) owns the *Daily Express*, the *Sunday Express*, the *Daily Star*, the *Yorkshire Post*, *Scottish Daily Express*, *Scottish Sunday Express* and eight regional dailies including those in Sheffield, Blackpool, Preston, Newport and two in Leeds. His other publishing interests include *Punch*, *Exchange & Mart* and many titles published by Benn, Morgan Grampian and YANG – The Yellow Advertising Newspaper Group which is the biggest independent publisher of free papers and is now turning to publishing paid-for weeklies as well. Tiny (Roland) Rowlands owns *The Observer*, the *Glasgow Herald* and a spread of provincial papers all over the country. Associated Newspapers run the *Daily Mail*, *The Mail on Sunday*, *The London Evening Standard*, provincial dailies in centres such as Derby, Hull, Leicester, Plymouth, Grimsby and Exeter, and more than a dozen weekly newspapers scattered round the country.

The provincial press

When it comes to circulation and readership figures (the latter on average 2.75 times higher than the former, according to the quarterly figures published by the Audit Bureau of Circulation), the regional and local press knock the nationals into a shredding machine. About 20 million people read a regional morning or evening newspaper, more than 25 million buy a local weekly paper, and most of them read both. At the latest count there are more than 1,850 provincial papers, including 90 morning and evening regional dailies, mostly published from city centres, 432 paid-for weeklies and an estimated 950 'freesheets', generally weeklies but some published less frequently. Gone are the days, moreover, when freesheets were considered below the salt and no self-respecting journalist would write for them; now, with few exceptions, they've pulled up their socks and worked hard to prove themselves worthy of everyone's market study. Between 1980 and 1989 circulation of freesheets increased by 24 million, and as their numbers have grown so has their image.

With the nationals concentrating on the national and international news flooding in from correspondents, news agencies and other sources, it is on regional and local events that the huge provincial press thrives. Should an important news story break in its circulation area a local paper will of course give the story closer coverage than national papers can – and the supporting features relevant to the story will be of enormous interest to local readers. But how, you may ask, is the freelance writer to be prepared for, say, an unexploded bomb being found in an old cellar, a local man winning £250,000 on the Premium Bonds, or a burglar breaking into a house and holding a family hostage for two days? Well, how do you think other writers rise to such challenges? Your file of press cuttings about your district just might be able to tell you if other old bombs have been found in the town, where, when, and what happened to them; the enterprising writer could have a collection of large-Premium Bond-winners' stories waiting for the right moment; information about other cases of families being held hostage in their homes will most certainly be dug out by somebody who writes the front page story in your local paper – so why shouldn't it be *you*? Incidentally, noting the differences in the way national, regional and local papers cover the same event – perhaps a major disaster – is a rewarding market study. If it's a story of more than local importance it ought to be you who writes it up for the régional paper as well; you will have all the facts ready at your fingertips, you will know the area and be able to contact the people involved.

Such is the popularity of regional dailies that Britain's most powerful, the *Manchester Evening News*, sells more copies a day than the *Financial Times*. All the leading evening papers can boast large circulation figures. More people buy *The London Evening Standard* every day than buy *The Times*; the *Birmingham Evening Mail*, the *Liverpool Echo* and Wolverhampton's *Express & Star* all sell in excess of 200,000 copies a day. Only slightly lower in circulation figures come the *Yorkshire Post* and the *Eastern Daily Press*. Top of the weeklies in this category is the *Western Gazette*, the biggest selling weekly in the country. Local Sunday provincial papers are also big sellers, the top two being Birmingham's *Sunday Mercury* and the *Sunday Sun* in Newcastle upon Tyne. Regional sections are planned or have been launched by several nationals; the *Daily Mirror* runs weekly regional sections in several areas of the country, including London, the Midlands, the North-East and Bristol. The *Leicester Mercury* has a special edition for Asians who make up 27% of the city's population.

In a special (and fragile) category are newspapers for children – *The Indy*, the *Early Times* (described as Britain's first quality newspaper for young people) and Glasgow's *Cult*. *Scoop* and several others have quietly faded away after brief and expensive lives, but still they tempt newspaper proprietors, the theory being that young readers gradually move up and become readers of the parent 'adult' paper. *The Guardian* prints a weekly page specially for young people. *The Times* delved into the finances of producing a junior supplement to be titled *The Thunderer* – and abandoned it. Now *The Daily Telegraph* is toying with the idea of launching their own paper for children. Watch this space, as some papers say to hook readers.

Here are some leading provincial papers, listed alphabetically: (all have six-figure circulations and many welcome freelance contributions; addresses are at the end of this chapter)

Aberdeen Press & Journal
Editor: Harry Roulston

Features editor: Norman Harper
Query the features editor first by letter. Features of 950 or 550 words are required, which must be relevant to north Scotland. They must also be topical. No light-hearted experiences, personal or otherwise. 'We prefer not to receive historical material because so few freelance writers handle it well, although we're willing to be convinced.' Pays £60 per thousand words.

Birmingham Evening Mail
Editor: Ian Dowell
Features editor: Paul Cole
Query first to Paul Cole. 'Few outside features required, notable exceptions showbiz interviews, features with West Midland angle. Payment varies.'

Bristol Evening Post
Editor: Adrian Faber
Features editor: Jim Keay
Pays NUJ rates but only a little freelance work is used – so it must be good!

Evening Chronicle (Newcastle upon Tyne)
Editor: Graeme Stanton
Prefers an initial approach in writing.

Evening News (Edinburgh)
Editor: Terry Quinn
Welcomes unsolicited feature material. Contact by phone preferred. Pays NUJ rates.

Evening Sentinel (Stoke on Trent)
Editor: Sean Dooley
Material welcomed and all should be sent to the News editor.

Express & Star (Wolverhampton)
Editor: Keith Parker
Features editor: Garry Copeland
Various requirements; phone first and speak to the news desk. Pays NUJ rates. Prompt and helpful to deal with.

Glasgow Daily Record
Editor: Endell J Laird
Features editor: Russell Steele

Contact features editor by phone first. Pays NUJ rates, minimum £93.50 per 1,000 words.

Glasgow Herald
Editor: Arnold Kemp
Deputy editor: Harry Reid
Exec. editor: Ron Anderson
Query deputy editor first by letter or phone. 'We use a considerable amount of freelance material, largely from long-standing contributors. But we are always in the market for high quality material.'

Leicester Mercury
Editor: Alex Leys
Experienced contributors should contact the editor first.

Liverpool Echo
Editor: John Griffith
Features editor: Paul Burnell
Query Paul Burnell by letter or phone (ext. 2512). 'We will consider any freelance submissions (though commissioned pieces are rare). Especially, though not exclusively, items with local (Merseyside) interest. The Echo is a "popular" provincial evening, so features need to be aimed at mass market interest, and generally no more than 1,000 words.' Payment by negotiation (average £40 for page lead). News stories are also welcome. News editor: Alf Green (ext. 2488/2499).

South Wales Echo
Deputy editor: Alan Gathergood
'We rarely use freelance material as our feature output is predominantly staff produced or agency orientated, regular or on spec. If a freelance does come up with a good idea that he or she can turn into a good piece, a telephone call to the features editor is a must.'

Sunday Mail (Glasgow)
Editor: Noel Young
Downmarket material for a large readership.

Sunday Post (Glasgow)
Editor: William Anderson
Has a circulation in excess of *one million*. All contributions to be sent directly to the Editor.

The London Evening Standard
Editor: John Leese
London-based material mostly required, but good opportunities exist for experienced writers at all times.

The Manchester Evening News
Editor: Michael Unger
Features editor: Ken Wood
Prompt and helpful. Requires wide ranging features with strong human and regional interest. Query the features editor by letter first. Payment according to NUJ agreement with the paper (see Chapter 8).

The Star (Sheffield)
Editor: Michael Corner
News editor: Martin Ross
Feature editor: Stuart Machin
Specialised features considered, and items relating to the area. Payment by negotiation.

Yorkshire Evening Post
Editor: Christopher Bye
A sister paper to the smaller-circulation *Yorkshire Post*. All contributions should be sent to the Editor.

Published market guides

Most marketing sections of publications designed to help writers deal with outlets for fiction and magazine articles but in their pages may also be some information about newspapers and their requirements. The main sources of market news are *The Writers' & Artists' Yearbook*, *The Writers' Handbook* and *Willings Press Guide* (see Chapter 6). Such sources as these are well-known and open to all writers, so competition for the papers they mention may be stiff. Make sure, of course, that all the references you consult are as up-to-date as possible.

Whereas you're not likely to miss the arrival (or closure) of a national paper (such is the publicity given to these events), you have to keep watch over newspaper births and deaths (and sometimes, marriages) in local and provincial journalism. Any local library should be able to tell you what is published to cover your area or the area you are interested in, but a more practical way of finding the very latest in local publishing is to ask your newsagent. Make him a friend and waylay him for a chat at a time he's not busy. He'll probably be delighted to find someone sufficiently interested in newspapers to ask him about them. A close notebook-in-hand study of his shelves, if nothing better, will give you local information. While published lists of titles and addresses inevitably date quickly, *British Rate and Data*, known in the business as 'BRAD', probably remains the UK's most reliable guide to circulation figures and readership profiles (see Chapter 6). Even when you've identified and located regional and local papers you're looking for, you can't relax; papers close, change their titles, disappear within their own groups or merge with former rivals.

Local papers

Whatever else local papers may be they are all intensely local in appeal. As you study them more closely you will realise 'local' does not necessarily mean 'narrow-minded' or 'parochial' in its pejorative sense. Broadly speaking they exist for three reasons: to strengthen community 'togetherness'; for instance, with pride in past or current achievements; to protect the community, say by highlighting shortcomings in local street-lighting, or allowing readers to voice protests about children's playgrounds; and (perhaps most important of the three) to inform readers. It almost goes without saying they must also interest and should frequently entertain them as well. The best papers work hard for their success; the *Bolton Evening News* is the first regional evening paper to run for 24 hours a day, seven days a week and no doubt more will follow.

As there are so many of them, local papers are the hardest to list; it's virtually impossible to detail what they want from freelance writers; yet of all newspaper markets they present the easiest target. You may be weary of the old advice, 'Study the market' but writing for local papers proves how essential it is. Read your local paper regularly and you can hardly help but get the 'feel' of it; you know how its mind works and you know what the reaction of the people who are reading it will be to its various parts. If this is 'market study' it's quite painless, isn't it? Call it *absorption* or *instinct* instead if you like. However it's described, this is the depth of knowing a market that shows you what and how to write for it.

It pays to think of your local paper not with an indulgent smile but as if it is talking to a friend, or a few thousand friends, as indeed it is. We have no difficulty in making casual conversation with our acquaintances about titbits of what's happening in the area, scraps of gossip and chatter of mutual interest, and we should feel equal ease with the 'local rag'. Just remember how distanced from it you felt when you first moved into the area or the scant interest you can summon when you read someone else's paper in a place you don't know. A local paper is exactly what it wants to be – something you can relax with, a good friend until you consign it to its after life of lighting the fire or wrapping up the fish and chips.

Find your own markets

Like other writers I've had cause for many years to be grateful to reference books but over and over again I have proved that nothing is more successful than finding markets for yourself; catch them in their infancy (experience and experimentation will sometimes tell you how viable they may be in the long term) and you've a good chance not only of 'getting in on the ground floor' but also of persuading the editor to mould the paper just a little in the way you would like it to go. Seeing your own column or page in every issue and knowing it's only there because you made it is a great boost to the confidence! Always be on the lookout for news in existing publications as well. This opener caught my eye in a writers' magazine: 'A series of 39 community newspapers has been launched in the Birmingham area in what could be the start of a new chapter in local newspaper publishing.' The story went on to give details of the expected date of publication, anticipated circulation figures and editorial content of all the papers. The closing quote from the editor is the most intriguing: 'We will have time to cover the kind of stories that other papers do not.' What an invitation to the waiting freelance, especially one in the circulation area! Does *your* head instantly fill with ideas for regular features, articles, original columns, or – at the very least – query letters to the editor? And does excitement mount as you get started on them?

Here's some more market news I spotted not long ago: the Kent Messenger Group of newspapers is now publishing (in English and French editions) a quarterly supplement called 'Rendezvous', to augment their existing stable of eight paid-for titles and 23 freesheets; the *Jersey Evening Post* is printing a lively (and, at the moment, viable) supplement for young readers, called *Reality*; Lancaster & Morecambe Newspapers have launched a weekly freesheet titled *The Reporter*, with no editorial staff whatsoever, filling its pages with stories from their other titles but (I'm sure) leaving a wide-open opportunity for the enterprising freelance. *The Profile* is a new (April 1990) title for Asians – their first national in this country. It is a weekly with a planned circulation of 15,000 and a cover price of 30 pence. The editor is Abdul Montaqim who is working with a staff of seven.

I don't mind at all giving you news of a few markets that may not as yet be widely known. Such is the fragility of new launches that by the time you read this they may, alas, have folded and in any case by then I will certainly have discovered more. So, I hope, will you.

Freesheets

In Great Britain we can expect (and often cannot *avoid*) an average of 42 million free papers pushed through our letterboxes at regular intervals. More than half of them are free 'extras' from the same stables as our paid-for weeklies, which is perhaps why the business of issuing both is known to the trade as 'total publishing'. The freesheets, or 'frees', vary greatly in size, quality and frequency of publication (although most are weeklies) and as in the national paper industry, ownership tends to be concentrated in the hands of a few large companies. The giants in the fields of both regional paid-for papers and freesheets are Thomson Regional Newspapers, Reed Regional Newspapers, Northcliffe Newspapers, United Newspapers and the Yellow Advertiser Newspaper Group.

The *A–Z of Britain's Free Newspapers and Magazines* is published every year by AFN (the Association of Free Newspapers and Magazines, see Chapter 6) listing some 600 titles and addresses, areas in which they circulate, the type of readership they aim to reach and other details. The papers may be free but this AFN annual survey is expensive; writing to AFN (and its sister organisation the Association of Free Magazines and Periodicals) may be the best way to obtain information, and either or both these associations may provide free copies of their current publications *AFN News* and *Free Magazine Review* if you explain your reasons for wanting to see them.

Free papers are read by 76% of all adults, compared to 43% for paid-for papers, and there are virtually as many openings for freelance writers in the freesheet pages as they have the ingenuity to produce. Where the paid-for weeklies will have established correspondents in most circulation areas (again, not all, so there are often openings there) freesheets largely depend on the man/woman-in-the-street for a supply of news, coverage of forthcoming events, topical and non-topical features and whatever else the enterprising writer may create. With no disrespect to the average men/women-in-the-street (certainly not, for they are the buyers of newspapers and without them we'd all be out of a job!), they have little idea this demand exists, and if they did they would have no notion of how to set about filling it. Bless them then, for in their blissful ignorance lies a freelance's opportunity: a glance at any freesheet page will readily reveal openings to the market-seeking eye of a determined contributor; closer careful study and some resourceful work will be the first step to supplying what is wanted.

If there are two or more freesheets covering your area or one you know, study them individually and together. Noting their likenesses and their differences will be invaluable. Incidentally, as the notion has died that writing for freesheets is beneath the 'real' journalist's dignity, so has that more distasteful idea that 'frees don't pay'; nowadays they most certainly do! Freesheets are big business and of course their writers should and do expect to be treated as 'proper' writers.

Special editions of national papers can define a catchment area, but it is hardly precise targeting. They are unable to aim at specific postcode areas and get to the local grassroots in the way frees can. *Leicester Mail*, for instance, is a free weekly micro-targeting in two editions aimed at specific parts of the city. The Group began micro-targeting a couple of years ago with editions of up to 8 local pages wrapped round the core newspaper.

With the numbers of freesheets increasing all the time (despite a relatively high casualty rate) they seem to have cornered the market on apt titles: the *Witney Blanket* is the first locally based free paper in Witney, Oxon., and there are no prizes for guessing the home base of the *Worcester Source* or the *Malvern Beacon*. More and more frees springing up all over the place is nothing but good news for freelance writers.

A grey area

There are newspapers and there are magazines (or 'periodicals' as they are confusingly called in the trade: aren't all publications periodical?). Everybody knows newspapers are printed in ink that quickly makes your fingers dirty on the type of paper referred to as 'newsprint' and that magazines are on thicker, glossier paper and have their pages stapled, sewn or stuck together. So what does that make the weekend colour supplements which have no existence separate from their big national parents? And what about all the papers/magazines devoted to readers of specialist trades or religious groups, material published by companies for their employees or hobbyist papers for enthusiasts? Many of these are printed on newsprint, but are they newspapers or magazines and should they come within the scope of this book? Some time ago I sold a regular column to the *Morning Advertiser*, the organ of the Licensed Victuallers' trade and the smallest national daily, but it is still commonly referred to as a 'magazine'. Since part of this book is applicable to magazines as well as to newspapers it would seem churlish to leave the 'grey' area on the copytaster's spike but to print a comprehensive listing of even the main 'greys' is impossible. I must leave it to the reader, therefore, to decide, in the process of becoming a writer, whether or not grey is beautiful. While some of the greys pay nothing and contributors would not expect otherwise, there is no doubt that there are circumstances in which going grey can be quite profitable.

Overseas markets, syndication and teletext

Once you get into the habit of looking for potential markets they pop up everywhere. Freelance opportunities abound in the overseas press and are to be found in relevant reference guides; some large overseas cities run English-language newspapers and syndication here and overseas of already published work can continue to earn smaller sums for writers ready to hand it over to syndication agencies. Published and unpublished work may also be syndicated here. See Chapter 7 for more about syndicating your work.

CEEFAX and ORACLE, the teletext information pages, are granted toeholds at the end of this chapter solely because they describe themselves as 'talking newspapers'. Say 'newspapers' and my nose twitches. They are systems using a television screen to display pages of news or other information chosen by the viewer who flicks from page to page in much the same way as turning the pages of a 'paper' newspaper. On an ordinary television picture that is not adjusted properly it is possible to see a few lines of what look like black and white spots at the top of the screen. These are, in fact, coded signals for CEEFAX (the BBC system) and ORACLE (IBA's) but a special adaptor is needed to decode them and show the 'pages' on the screen. They present an unusual but not impenetrable market for freelance writers, several of whom have their own specialist pages or mini-series screened regularly.

Newspaper addresses

NATIONAL DAILIES:

Daily Express

Head Office:	Ludgate House
	245 Blackfriars Road
	London SE1 9UX
Tel:	071 928 8000
Fax:	071 633 0244

Daily Mail

Head Office:	Northcliffe House
	2 Derry Street
	London W8 5TT
Tel:	071 938 6000
Fax:	071 937 3251

Daily Mirror

Head Office:	Holborn Circus
	London EC1P 1DQ
Tel:	071 353 0246
Fax:	071 822 3405

Daily Star

Head Office:	Ludgate House
	245 Blackfriars Road
	London SE1 9UX
Tel:	071 928 8000
Fax:	071 620 1641

Financial Times

Head Office:	1 Southwark Bridge London SE1 9HL
Tel:	071 873 3000
Fax:	071 407 5700

Morning Star

Head Office:	74 Luke Street London EC2A 4PY
Tel:	071 939 6166

The Daily Telegraph

Head Office:	Peterborough Court South Quay 181 Marsh Wall London E14 9SR
Tel:	071 538 5000
Fax:	071 538 3810

(Moving to Canada Square, Canary Wharf, Docklands, 1992)

The Guardian

Head Office:	119 Farringdon Road London EC1
Tel:	071 278 2332

The Independent

Head Office:	40 City Road London EC1Y 2DB
Tel:	071 253 1222
FREEFONE:	only on application
Fax:	various

The Sun

Head Office:	PO Box 481 Virginia Street London E1 9BD
Tel:	071 782 4000
Fax:	071 488 3253

The Times

Head Office:	1 Pennington Street London E1 9XN
Tel:	071 782 5000

Today
Head Office: 70 Vauxhall Bridge Road
                                      London SW1 2RP
Tel: 071 630 1300
Fax: 071 630 6839

SUNDAYS:

Sunday Express
Head Office: Ludgate House
                                      245 Blackfriars Road
                                      London SE1 9UX
Tel: 071 928 8000
Fax: 071 922 7964

Sunday Mirror
Head Office: 33 Holborn
                                      London EC1P 1DQ
Tel: 071 353 0246

Sunday Sport
Head Office: Marten House
                                      39–47 East Road
                                      London N1 6AH
Tel: 071 251 2544

The Mail on Sunday
Head Office: Northcliffe House
                                      2 Derry Street
                                      London W8 5TT
Tel: 071 938 6000
FREEFONE: 0800 010111
Fax: 071 937 3829

The News of the World
Head Office: 1 Virginia Street
                                      London E1 9BD
Tel: 071 782 4000
FREEFONE: 0800 010373
Fax: 071 583 9504

The People
Head Office: Holborn Circus
                                      London EC1P 1DQ
Tel: 071 353 0246
Fax: 071 822 3405/3684

Sunday Telegraph

Head Office:	Peterborough Court
	South Quay
	181 Marsh Wall
	London E14 9SR
Tel:	071 538 5000
Fax:	071 538 1330

(Moving to Canada Square, Canary Wharf, Docklands, 1991)

The Independent on Sunday

Head Office:	40 City Road
	London EC1
Tel:	071 253 1222
Fax:	071 415 1333

The Observer

Head Office:	Chelsea Bridge House
	Queenstown Road
	London SW8 4NN
Tel:	071 627 0700
Fax:	071 627 5570–2

The Sunday Times

Head Office:	1 Pennington Street
	London E1 9XW
Tel:	071 782 5000
Fax:	071 782 5658

PROVINCIAL PAPERS:

Aberdeen Press & Journal

Head Office:	Lang Stracht
	Aberdeen AB9 8AF
Tel:	0224 690222
Fax:	0224 699575

Belfast Telegraph

Head Office:	Royal Avenue
	Belfast BT1 1EB
Tel:	0232 321242
Fax:	0232 242287

Birmingham Evening Mail
Head Office: 28 Colmore Circus
                                     Queensway
                                     Birmingham B4 6AY
Tel: 021 236 3366
Fax: 021 233 0271

Bristol Evening Post
Head Office: Temple Way
                                     Old Market
                                     Bristol BS99 7HD
Tel: 0272 863053
Fax: 0702 279568

Evening Chronicle
Head Office: Thomson House
                                     Groat Market
                                     Newcastle upon Tyne
                                     NE1 1ED
Tel: 091 232 7500

Evening Sentinel
Head Office: Sentinel House
                                     Etruria
                                     Stoke on Trent
                                     Staffs ST1 5SS
Tel: 0782 289800

Express & Star
Head Office: Queen Street
                                     Wolverhampton WV1 3BU
Tel: 0902 313131
Fax: 0902 21467

Glasgow Daily Record
Head Office: Anderston Quay
                                     Glasgow G3 8DA
Tel: 041 248 7000
FREEFONE (for copy):   0800 393 123
Fax: 041 204 0703

Glasgow Herald
Head Office: 195 Albion Street
                                     Glasgow G1 1QP
Tel: 041 552 6255
Fax: 041 552 2288

Leicester Mercury

Head Office:	St Georges Street
	Leicester LE1 9QF
Tel:	0533 512512

Liverpool Echo

Head Office:	PO Box 48
	Old Hall Street
	Liverpool L69 3EB
Tel:	051 227 2000
Fax:	051 236 4682

South Wales Echo

Head Office:	Western Mail & Echo Ltd
	Thomson House
	Havelock Street
	Cardiff CF1 1WR
Tel:	0222 223333

Sunday Mail

Head Office:	Anderston Quay
	Glasgow G8 8DA
Tel:	041 248 7000
Fax:	041 242 3145

Sunday Post

Head Office:	144 Port Dundas Road
	Glasgow G4 0HZ
Tel:	041 332 9933
Fax:	041 331 1595

The London Evening Standard

Head Office:	Northcliffe House
	2 Derry Street
	London W8 5TT
Tel:	071 938 6000

Manchester Evening News

Head Office:	164 Deansgate
	Manchester M60 2RD
Tel:	061 832 7200
Fax:	061 839 0968

The Star
Head Office: York Street
                            Sheffield S1 1PU
Tel: 0742 767676
Fax: 0742 753551

Yorkshire Evening Post
Head Office: Wellington Street
                            Leeds LS1 1RF
Tel: 0532 432701
Fax: 0532 443430

OTHERS:

Early Times
Head Office: 95 Ditchling Road
                            Brighton
                            East Sussex BN1 4SE
Tel: 0273 675374
Fax: 0273 692081

The European
Head Office: Orbit House
                            5 New Fetter Lane
                            London EC4A 1AP
Tel: 071 822 2002
Fax: 071 377 4891

3
What to Write

Not what-to-write-*about*

This chapter is a guide to what types of writing newspapers may need but doesn't dwell on what to write about. A list of suitable topics would (a) fill the rest of the book, and (b) scarcely be topical as I have no way of knowing what's going to be in the news and public awareness when you read this. Although you may be prepared to devote much effort and research to a project and bring originality to it, mere lists of ideas can encourage stultified and channelled thinking from the start. Countless writers before you have stared at similar lists and tried to wrench the last gasp of inspiration from them; countless editors have seen (and rejected) the results. More is needed than an idea. A unique slant may be a pointer to a worthwhile venture but an idea is most likely to be successful when it arrives in your head jockeying for priority, albeit loosely at first, with a notion of how you're going to write it. When you can look at them both objectively, i.e. when you can distance yourself sufficiently from what you intend to write or have written, the idea may strike you as old hat after all; we all have faces of two eyes, a nose and a mouth but, identical twins apart, they're all different. Isn't it amazing (and a blessing) that it's possible to have so many interpretations of the same idea, a boring old face? It's the same with writing; just as the personality behind your face makes it different from anyone else's, so the viewpoint, attitude, treatment, tone, mood, voice, the *character* behind an idea will make it yours alone. An elderly journalist once said to me: 'Don't write anything anyone else can write.' Wise words indeed.

People who know nothing about writing imagine we only write what we want to write. We can pick and choose, they presume, and of course not write anything we don't want to. Nobody's making us do it, after all. That would be an adequate philosophy for a writer with an annual output of a couple of Letters to the Editor, say, or a once-yearly report in a local charity booklet. 'Tea-time' writers can indulge in the luxury of choosing how much to write and what to write about – and good luck to every one. If you're in this writing business as a serious endeavour you'll have a totally different approach. A fisherman baits his hook not with what he likes, but with what fish like. There are many hard lessons to learn about freelancing and one of the toughest is that you have to write not just the stories that appeal to you, but the stories that will sell. When you enjoy working on those as well (and if you're a journalist at heart, you will, believe me) that can only be counted as a bonus.

Whatever laws are quoted as paths to success one is supreme and irrefutable: the only certain entrée to the columns of a newspaper is a good story, well written. If you constantly remind yourself that it's what readers want that sells, you will instinctively know what to give them because (if for no other reason) it's probably what you want for yourself. Good health, a happy marriage or relationship, to earn and save enough money, to own a nice house and most of the material goods you want (within reason), to have other people respect and admire you, to have a good job and do well in it, to safeguard your children – are these not common aims and desires of the great general public? Most of us, wishing no harm or hardship to others, care most about self-interest. Write about that natural wish among readers, especially telling them how to satisfy it, and you'll always give them what they want to read. And when readers want it, editors buy it. Readers may think they dislike change, but they want originality. News and design are inseparable parts of a good newspaper, yet when a *Guardian* reader heard that part of the paper was to be redesigned, he immediately wrote to the editor: 'I don't like it.' That may be an instinctive response to the prospect of change, especially among older readers, but research into newspaper readership before and after even major changes indicates most readers of all age groups remain loyal. You can be sure papers would change very little were that not so, for there is nothing to be gained by attracting new readers if you lose an equal number of existing ones – or more.

It is only sensible to start with the markets that want freelance material and say so. There are many actually asking for it if you know where to look. The news items or job opportunities columns of trade papers and magazines for professional journalists often advertise their need for freelances because this, they know, is where professional freelances will look for markets. The *UK Press Gazette* and *Journalist's Week* (see Chapter 6) are the two best known. Opening one at random as I write I see: 'Freelance district reporter wanted, Somerset and Avon area, to dig out splashes, human interest stories, parish pars and features.' Another wants a part-time writer to research and write articles for an in-house magazine for a large manufacturing company in the food industry. A third says: 'Freelance feature writers wanted, with the ability to write lively and informative copy on a wide range of topics.' Elsewhere I read a plea for village correspondents for the *Western Morning News*, the regional daily in Plymouth and the South-West. You don't have to be a full-time writer, remember, or a union member to qualify for that 'professional' tag; you do have to be (or at least it helps if you are) professional in your work.

A better place to look, of course, is the most logical place of all – the market itself. Items reviewing the day's or week's newspapers are sometimes featured on television and can be useful guides but there is no real substitute for studying the papers you'd like to write for. Analyse their content, their page layout and format and try to find out why they print the features/news items/fillers (or whatever you are interested in) that they do. Even this market study isn't infallible, for at best it can only reveal what they printed and were interested in *yesterday*. As for what they'll want tomorrow and the next day and the next.... No matter where you live or work, whom you meet, how you spend your time or what your hobbies and interests may be, there's a story. Feature, filler, news item, article, review, regular series, specialist column, interview, diary item, letter, anecdote, profile, preview; there is always something to be written.

When you start selling work you will get to know the likes and dislikes of individual editors but editors don't occupy the same seats for ever, so keep an eye on who is moving jobs. Mr A's approach to space filling may be quite different from Mr B's. Editor X may reply promptly and pay at the end of the current month; editor Z may be hard to contact and capricious about money. One paper I wrote for over a six year period kept its contributors at a distance. In all that time I spoke to neither the editor nor anyone on his staff; my copy was published precisely as I submitted it, without any apparent subbing, until I felt if I just sent in a few pages of a telephone directory there they would be, faithfully reproduced, in the next issue of the paper. (My smugness was inevitably shattered; such a strange working method means mistakes go in too, and mine did; it taught me to be more careful.) It was a delightful paper to work for. Cheques arrived on time, the pay was pleasantly increased at suitable intervals without comment – and then I received an invitation to a retirement party. The editor was leaving (a shy man, I discovered, who thought writers should be left alone to write) and a new one was appointed. Wow! His approach to the job was entirely different; letters and memos whizzed back and forth and 'regulars' had to change their habits. Not a bad thing, perhaps, for nothing stays the same for long on newspapers, and they're usually all the better for that.

The most common reason for the replacement of an editor is not his retirement, but that he wants to move or his employers feel the paper could do with a new face at the helm and a different hand on the tiller. To find out what a new editor likes watch the paper closely when he takes over, and keep watching it for several weeks as he may have to convince his superiors before he can incorporate the changes he'd like. They will probably only need convincing over changes in general direction; it is rare for editorial boards or proprietors to interfere with the daily or weekly content or tone of a paper. New editor or not, don't write and ask for a sheet of guidelines (which many magazines are happy to supply) unless you want to be considered too lazy to do your own market study and too slow and amateurish for a weekly paper, let alone a daily. And before we leave the subject of editors, remember it is often profitable to 'follow' one you're used to working for. Just as a new broom will tend to sweep clean in his old seat, so he may be the new broom somewhere else ready to turn to you in gratitude if he knows he has been able to rely on you in the past for good, reliable copy when he wants it.

Whatever you write, never forget the purpose of doing so. Plan an article about how to grow chrysanthemums in straw, for example, and ask yourself why you are writing it. It's a means to an end. Readers don't want to know how to grow chrysanthemums in straw; they want perfect chrysanthemums. When you feature a bright summary of the latest kitchen gadgets remind yourself they don't want the gadgets: they want the benefits that come from using them. In buying a paper (or a magazine) readers instinctively ask themselves, 'What's in it for me?' You are providing the answer.

Never turn away a commission or a chance to work on a story because you don't know anything about the subject. An editor asked me to fill in for another writer who had been taken ill and write about a band of duck-devotees holding up the traffic to let squads of ducks cross the road in safety from one part of a country park to another. Many times I'd seen ducks gathering at a particular spot by the side of the road and had prayed they would stay there. But I had no idea they were trained to wait until their personal crossing wardens arrived to see them to the other side. Adopting one of the tenets of a journalist's craft and never being afraid to ask anyone for information, I discovered the local police could not grant official permission to the kindly patrols when they wanted to hold up the traffic but had promised they would only take action against them if motorists complained about being asked to stop. The duck-devotees had done their teaching job well; so impeccably behaved were their quacking charges in waddling across that motorists were only amused and intrigued. My story (and some pix) in the local paper (and further afield) ensured everyone in the area knew about the web-footed crossing patrols. Extra volunteers joined the others in shepherding the ducks and someone suggested there should be a crossing sign showing a little green duck when it was safe to cross. It was all harmless fun which everyone enjoyed as much as I did.

On less frivolous topics you may need to do a proportion of your work before ever writing a word. A thinly researched article quickly lands on the reject pile if another author has taken more time and trouble to delve into the subject. That's what reference libraries are for, and there are enormous facilities for researching anything and everything (see Chapter 6). What's more, as your pile of researched material grows so will your interest and enthusiasm. To write well you have to be interested in what you're writing, or at least make yourself interested. If you're not, why should anyone else be?

An escape from a topic you're bored with? An esoteric subject that suddenly intrigues you? A story whose main attraction is that it's what you've always wanted to write? Beware. These can be reasons for your story not selling because they're the wrong reasons for writing it. Are you therefore condemning yourself to nothing but monotony and feigned interest? By no means. There are some fortuitous results of getting stuck into this freelancing business; success is more consistent when you persevere and the more you do, the more you find you're enjoying it. Many years ago a journalist with worldwide experience and credits to match advised me thus: 'Streams of workable ideas come only to those constantly engaged in creative work.' Those workable ideas are what we want to write, but first they must be what readers want to read.

A newspaper may be only ink on paper but it's alive; luckier than the gadfly with its three hours, and sometimes given a whole fortnight or even longer. It feeds on the topicality and originality its makers can give it, and on the quality of the writing on its pages. Aim to please the readers and the editor will also be pleased because he wants the same thing, although many I've come across admit they don't know what they want until they see it.

There are other folk with an essential part to play in the business of newspapers, and they are the advertisers.

Learn from the adverts

You'll recall from the first chapter about how a newspaper is put together that the advertisements are always positioned before anything else. There are several reasons why this is so and the crude fact that advertisers are paying the paper, i.e. buying the space their advertisements occupy, is the primary one, although many newspaper proprietors would have you believe in more altruistic reasons. Undoubtedly the money received from advertisers, especially the big regular spenders, is the life blood of newspapers, but the true value of advertising can be assessed only in awareness of other considerations. The wider the spread of papers the more outlets there are for an advertiser's message and the stronger becomes his bargaining power, although his feedback from readers is more difficult to record. There is no doubt, however, that advertisers are even more easily blown about by the fortunes of the times than are newspapers themselves. The country's overall economic position will give an indication of the current health of the newspaper business; is a recession round the corner, are interest rates high, is unemployment rising? Matters way outside the newspaper world can have an inevitable (and sometimes devastating) effect on it. They will affect all papers (yes, your local weekly as well) to a greater or lesser degree, depending on how much they rely on selling their advertising space.

British newspapers are not subsidised although they are

zero-rated for VAT. If they didn't accept advertising their cover prices would be high, sales would be low and many would go out of business. So their income depends on two sources, advertising revenue and sales; in what proportion will depend on several factors. The popular papers have less need to rely on ad revenue than have their more serious competitors.

These are some of the most recently released proportions of advertising/sales figures:

Percentage of income from	advertising	sales
The Sun (popular daily)	27	73
Sunday Mirror (popular Sunday)	31	69
The Guardian (quality daily)	58	42
The Observer (quality Sunday)	66	34
Yorkshire Post (regional daily)	61	39
Western Gazette	84	16

In some cases there may be special influences at work as well: the speedy collapse of Communism in much of eastern Europe at the end of the 1980s, for instance, dealt a severe blow to the *Morning Star*. When the Soviet Union cut its order by 6,000 copies a day pagination was reduced from 12 to eight pages, the editorial staff was cut from 40 to 28 and the paper faced an annual £400,000 loss of income. Advertising space is not likely to sell well in a paper experiencing such troubled times. And if advertisers don't support the paper....

The free papers are most dependent on selling advertising space. It is their sole source of income and few can survive for long with falling revenue and an economically pessimistic prognosis. But their very vulnerability is also their strength: they can target readership more accurately and they may respond to revenue difficulties more rapidly and with greater versatility than paid-for local weeklies in the same areas. Despite a slightly lower advertising growth rate in 1990 than in the previous year, the long-term forecast in this field is bright. Training, design, improved distribution and better quality in editorial matter are seen as the key factors in keeping the free papers vigorous and in good health. Note 'better quality in editorial matter': that promises freelances as well as staff writers that standards will rise. A writer friend of mine laughingly recounts telling another of her success in a local publication. 'That's a good market,' was the second writer's reply. 'They'll take anything.' Not quite the compliment the speaker intended it to be, perhaps, but don't think that higher standards make freelancing more difficult for the very reverse is true; the higher the standards the fewer are the writers able to write well enough for publication, so the competition is less, not more. Let the challenge of higher standards bring out the best in your working ability.

For valuable market study read newspaper advertisements carefully; they've cost the advertisers large sums (a full-page ad in *The Sun* currently costs £26,000) and advertisers don't spend that money without careful reader-targeting. Actually the work of researching the potential profitability of placing advertisements and the buying of the advertising space will not have been undertaken by big newspaper companies themselves but by the advertising agencies they employ. The agencies depend for their fees on the success of their work, i.e. readers' response to the ads they place, which is carefully monitored. If the agencies don't get it right they, as well as their customers, will suffer and next time the customers will use another agency. So a good agency keen to satisfy and retain the folk who pay their bills will have done a great deal of professional research and taken pains to ensure their advertisements will be put before the eyes of readers with particular proclivities and life styles; freelances can benefit from trying to see the readers through the same eyes.

Editors may protest that they are never influenced by advertisements (which assertions can hardly please the advertisers) but writers may do well by remembering where the paper's money is coming from. More than once I've imagined I was one of the advertisers wanting to write editorial copy (it is strictly unethical for them to do so, of course) and sold features helpful to people already interested in the advertisements; an extension of them, if you like, but one that mentions no actual product and is not identified with any particular advertisement or company. A paper strong on ads for young mothers, for instance, welcomed copy about working mothers hiring daytime childminders. As a bonus, by the way, I received a basketful of baby foods and toiletries from an appreciative advertiser; it seemed churlish to mention my own children were then into their teens so a younger friend had a lucky surprise. Another weekly paper keen on publicising correspondence schools wanted my feature on the advantages of learning by mail in your own home. (Without knocking the value of correspondence courses, I was relieved when nobody offered me a free one in anything.)

So how is the freelance to interpret what the advertisements reveal about the readers? Agencies have it coldly cut-and-dried and work on a clear idea of where we all fit into today's society. They've assessed what sort of people the readers will be and the advertisements they place will reflect that estimated socioeconomic class. Of course not all readers fall into the same group in every respect; there will always be left-wing supporters reading *The Daily Telegraph* and die-hard traditionalists liking the *News of the World* so the best even advertising agencies can do is aim at a general assessment of readership.

Like it or not, we all fall into one or other of these so-called 'socioeconomic' groups, for reference divided into A, B, C1, C2, D and E. We are placed in a 'group' by a practical evaluation of age, occupation, education, background, the type of house we live in, the car we drive, the holidays we choose etc. If we are not precisely categorised by income, capital and, most importantly, spending power, such details may be assumed from the rest of the classification. Typical C2s, for instance, are truck drivers, television repairmen or garage mechanics; skilled men and women who work with their hands but have had some officially recognised training or apprenticeship. The needs of this particular group are worth studying, incidentally, for they make up the country's largest single occupational category – 28% of all workers – and over 40% of them are buying their own homes compared to 35% of the entire population. Look at the car advertisements in any paper and you'll quickly see what the readership is estimated to be. BMWs or Ford Fiestas? And for shopping: the House of Fraser or Kays catalogue?

Features

The word 'article' is one you'll seldom hear on the editorial floor in most newspaper offices. Copy that might be referred to as an 'article' is more likely to be called a 'feature'. A feature is not an article made to sound grand for the terms are virtually synonymous. I make the point here only to clarify what a features editor or someone on his staff is almost certainly talking about when he refers to a 'feature', an 'article' or even a 'feature article'. In this book I use the first two terms and confess the tautologous third bewilders me.

Staff on newspapers tend to assume that a feature is copy written by a journalist whose work is well-known to readers through appearing in the paper regularly or frequently. It is more likely to include his informed point of view on the topic because, goes the logic, readers feel at home with the writer and understand him. Being regarded as almost a friend the feature writer deftly balances his innate emotional response to whatever he is writing with his practical training of how to write it most effectively. Not that all readers approve of his words, of course, but if they provoke lively discussion in Letters to the Editor, so much the better. The feature writer is someone whose work readers want to read, warts and all, a part of the paper they like and perhaps one of the main reasons why they keep buying it.

A series of single articles (or even one standing alone) may also be spoken of as a 'feature' since anyone writing it (you?) will by implication be something of an expert on the topic. Naturally a 'one-off' article has just as valid a place in a paper as anything else the editor wants to print and I regret the assumption I've occasionally encountered from inexperienced freelances that an 'article' is a minor piece expected merely to skim over the subject with two or three well-known or ill-researched facts, the writer's personal opinion and a lot of lightweight chitchat. Nothing will get published with that half-hearted benchmark – and it doesn't deserve to.

Call it what you wish, anything you send to the features editor of a newspaper needs to stop him in his tracks ('We must buy this') or at least lure him enough to contact you about development of a point here, getting a pic for a par there and so on. A further characteristic of a feature is that it is usually tagged to a news event. It may, for instance, give background information on a running story about prison rioting when there's been trouble at a nearby prison, reveal past histories of an unusual medical condition recently occurring in the district, or dig out some awkward facts following the disappearance of funds from a local charity's coffers. Whatever its theme, be careful your story is not out of date, having been overtaken by more recent news.

You may have already interested the editor or features editor with an exploratory letter but if you go in 'cold' it is even more important to hit him right between the eyes. You've made yourself an expert, remember, even if only a temporary one. Features may be based entirely on facts, but it is their relevance to *people* that makes them viable. Write a piece about the first impressions of eastern Europeans on seeing the shops in the West, with plenty of human interest and quotes, of course, or the increase in business for UK seaside hotel landladies due to high mortgage rates and airport hold-ups. Make yourself the bringer of comfort, an inspiration, an instructor or a wallower in nostalgia. Give readers the latest facts about education, medical services, local transport, job opportunities; all are important to people. There truly is no end to what you may write about. Of course the old advice given to beginners is still pertinent: 'Write about what you know.' But that doesn't mean fill your piece with little more than your own opinion and personal experiences. It is boring to be in the company of someone who talks about nothing but himself. Readers are interested in how what they're reading will relate to themselves!

It pays to look ahead; particularly in ways other writers may not. The traditional events on which countless hopefuls 'tag' their articles may be easy to write about but are often difficult to sell simply because they may have been sucked dry and written to death. Original freelance copy on an editor's desk is more welcome than a tea-break. As I write this the Broadcasting Bill going through Parliament is expected to ease the *Radio Times* and *TV Times* stranglehold on television listings. Every British newspaper is watching closely and planning to get in on what should be a lucrative new challenge. Thoughtful freelances are doing the same. Material about people in the public eye, radio and television writers, stars, presenters, producers and anyone who is a 'name' in the media will be piling onto the desks of feature writers everywhere, for a large amount of additional copy will surely be wanted to fill the new listings titles. Once you get your mind in gear, finding what to write about at the right time will never be a problem.

A good feature writer can write about virtually anything. When you do so make it strong; make them laugh, cry, want to know more, swear, feel encouraged, understand something or someone better, agree, disagree – or whatever you choose – but make sure they do or feel *something*. That's what feature writing is all about.

News

Have you heard the tale of Jack and Pete who were playing golf together on a small green when they saw an amateur player score a hole-in-one three times in a few minutes? After congratulations had flowed in the clubhouse Jack went home and told his wife about this remarkable feat over lunch. Pete didn't bother with the party in the clubhouse but hastily scribbled a few notes on the back of an envelope he found in his pocket and went straight to the nearest telephone. Local, regional and national papers paid handsomely for his story and would have paid a good deal more if he had also had a camera in his pocket at the time. The story was taken up by radio and television and earned headlines on all the sporting pages. Jack hasn't got and probably doesn't want a 'news-nose': Pete's is developing well and will surely lead him onto bigger and better stories he'll be more prepared to exploit to the full when they occur. Most importantly, he's learned the value of timing when it comes to filing a news story. News makes up only 10% of the space available in tabloids but a good deal more in the quality papers, so if you were Pete which of the nationals would you sell the story to after you'd let the local and regional papers have it?

Developing a news-nose isn't difficult if you are already keenly interested in people, what they do and what happens to them. In fact, once you get into the habit of spotting news you'll discover there's so much of it as to be an *embarrass des riches*. Then comes the art of selection, which also improves with experience of the markets waiting for news and an understanding of the value of each potential news item.

Seizing opportunities is one thing but you have to spot them first. Have you ever heard a friend telling a third party about something unusual he'd seen when you were with him, and you realise you hadn't noticed it? I have, and it warns me my sense of observation has been slipping. Practise training your eyes to notice what's going on around you, especially small and at first sight unimportant things (although not missing the larger ones either) and then – instinctively, with time – bring everything down to news-nose level for quick appraisal and selection. A successful news reporter not only sees things other people miss, he knows what to do with an unexpected news story.

If you are at the scene of an accident or an emergency this well-honed observation sense can prove invaluable, not only to you doing a job of work, but also to police, firemen, ambulancemen and anyone able to help unfortunate victims. Of course you will take notes as copiously and quickly as you can in the circumstances; then comes the writing of the story (see 'How to Write It') and getting it to the paper.

When speed is essential you will initially be guided by the deadline of your paper. If you are writing a news story for a regional evening paper, say, and it is ten o'clock in the morning the phone is the only practical way of filing copy. Find a telephone (a box for relative quietness and privacy, if possible), assemble your notes if you haven't had time to write the whole story and ring the paper. Presumably you will know the Freefone or ordinary number so ask at once for the News Desk. Local papers will probably not have anywhere in the office manned solely for news so tell whoever answers the phone that you have a news story for a copytaker. Anyone who can take copy over the phone should be able to get your story down. Submitting a news story to a paper with no imminent deadline is a less fraught affair but news about something that by the time of publishing will be several days old is also less useful to a freelance. In the intervening time all papers will have had their own staff cover any newsworthy stories. It may be hectic, but from the freelance's point of view the best news is that which happens at the right time – when it is inconvenient or too late for staff reporters to cover it!

Some can be bizarre. A village near my home has a long-standing grudge that there is no gas service to the villagers, although a gas main pipe runs beside the village street. Early one evening as I drove along it on my way to a theatre reviewing job in the small town some five miles further ahead, there was a tremendous explosion. The dust cleared to reveal a huge hole gaping by the village street where two old cottages had been. They had disappeared as if some giant hand had bent down and scooped them up. Police and ambulancemen quickly established there had – amazingly – been nobody in either cottage and there was no loss of life in the village; traffic was diverted round country lanes and policemen ran to every other dwelling warning that all fires must be extinguished immediately. A strong smell of gas hung in the air; the village that wanted gas had certainly got it. Satisfied that not even a dog or cat had been hurt, I realised the story was mine. It was not anything to rock the United Nations, but albeit less than earth-shattering (though in the literal sense that's exactly what it was), it was an exclusive front page news story. The theatre? Fortunately it was the first of a four-night run and a couple of quick phone calls deferred the job to the next evening.

On another occasion a serving Prime Minister's light plane was diverted to a small airfield because of bad weather and he scurried across the windy tarmac to precisely where I happened to be standing. That's another story that gave me the front page in the nationals as well as the locals. To have a photographer with you at such times (or to be one yourself) is a gift, and a picture of a bemused Prime Minister clearly not knowing where he'd landed in the country he was engaged in running was too good to miss.

Once you get into the habit of looking for news you'll find it seems to be looking for you. There is plenty around and on occasions it actually demands your attention. Be sure it deserves it! I'm reminded of a time when I was waiting for a friend outside a small Post Office and idly noticed a boy of about ten also waiting by a bakery on the other side of the road. We were at the foot of a steep deserted hill and as I lolled in the autumn sun there was a high-pitched scream from higher up. I glanced up to see a pram with a bundle in it rolling down the pavement towards the bakery. With hardly any effort and but one small side step, the waiting boy halted the pram and impassively held it while the breathless mother hurtled down the hill to grab it. My friend arrived at that moment and out of the corner of my eye I saw the mother reassure herself the baby was all right and turn to hug the boy.

Imagine my surprise at the front page lead story in the local paper: *'Boy Saves Baby in Daring Rescue – Risks Own Life'* etc. Hmm. I never discovered who the story came from but I learned a lot that day: above all, I learned what is and what is not news. That certainly wasn't and should never have been filling the front page or any other page because it wasn't true. I know. I was there. It may strike you as horrible that good fortune, in this case the safety of a baby, should be considered too trivial to be 'news' and you may be driven to think that if the world of news and newspapers is only concerned with death and disaster you want nothing to do with it. That would be a pity, for despite much of it seeming trite, the honest reporting of news does a great deal of good: it brings praise where it is due and rewards where they are deserved; worthwhile causes may be given valuable publicity; injustice can be highlighted; innocent people warned of dangers and, most important at all levels, readers can know they are being told the truth.

News writing can be dramatic but frequently it is writing about something that is anticipated: a report of a Council meeting, for instance, where an important decision is awaited affecting a keenly felt local issue. The meeting may come in the realm of general run-of-the-mill reporting and you may be there as an informal observer having made no prior contact with any paper to report anything. (You may also have taken the trouble to establish that there will be nobody else 'covering' for the press either, so your field is clear if anything newsworthy occurs.) Then, perhaps, a shouting match develops between opposing camps, some Council stalwarts walk out in disgust, someone accuses councillors of rigging the ballot on the issue in question or the decision itself is hard to believe. Those are the times when you'll not be just writing a report but filing a news story, and if there is a paper coming out the next morning you, as a freelance, could find yourself the only person able to write it. It was a news story that would have gone unheeded and unreported without your quick-wittedness.

Local correspondents

Do you fancy life as a reporter? These are the hard-working folk at the very root of a paper's activities. They are likely to be out and about collecting information from tip-offs supplied by the office, waiting to file the latest news on a 'running' story or they might be carrying out any one of a dozen duties in the circulation area. It's considered to be the foot of the ladder in the newspaper world but it's the place where many a leading journalist began learning the craft. A reporter carries considerable responsibility. He may be fresh out of training school or an older, more experienced writer who doesn't want to change his job; regardless of age, on papers covering a wide geographical area, he's probably overworked as well.

It is in just such circumstances that a freelance may find an opening. Weeklies in country districts especially, cannot hope to find out what is happening in every town and village every week and many events will go unreported (to the dissatisfaction of readers) unless somebody takes care of the community. It's a challenging job and one that should not be undertaken without careful consideration. Being committed to maintaining a flow of news from a small town or village or district can be a chore when you want to go on holiday or if you are ill, or if you suddenly don't feel like doing it. You may be a volunteer, or perhaps you were cajoled into doing it and didn't like to refuse, but the first rule of the job is that you don't let your community down.

Doing the 'calls' will be a regular task. This means you will call on the people or organisations likely to tell you what's going on: the Police and Fire stations, local hospitals, the Town Hall, the Citizens Advice Bureau, the morgue, the courts, schools, health clinics, community centres – anywhere and everywhere in the locality where a spokesman is able and willing to give you news or the basis of a news story to pass on to readers of the paper. How often you do the calls will depend on how often the paper is published, but with luck you'll soon find you have built up such a good network of contacts that some of them will be happy to contact you when they have anything to report. Far from being a bore, it can be one of the most fascinating tasks for a freelance to do, and will almost certainly bring you more rewards than cash (that word 'volunteer', I need hardly add, doesn't mean you are doing it for nothing).

You like the sound of it? As a welcome byproduct, your writing skills will benefit out of all proportion to the apparently humdrum level of the job. Making quick decisions about your copy, learning how to present it clearly in print and over the phone, developing good handwriting (you'll need to be sure you can read it yourself!), an increasing awareness about what is and what is not newsworthy, and a growing confidence in your own ability as a journalist make this a worthwhile job for a freelance at any stage of his career.

Finally, for countless readers the local reporter is the only 'real' journalist they see or ever will see, so on you will their opinion of the newspaper depend. Illogical and slightly daunting this may be but it is an extra reason for a freelance to do the job well and gain great satisfaction from it.

Specialist features and columns

Many freelances vow the best spot in a paper is a regular page/ half page/column/corner all to themselves. This type of work has been one of my specialities for more years than I can recall and I can vouch for the advantages of it. It is an arrangement that usually results from an approach made to an editor by the writer able to show convincing evidence of his ability to hold down a regular place in the paper. It's not a commission won without effort, often over a number of years; the editor will want to know you will be able to sustain an unlimited time at the job, that your copy will constantly be fresh and innovative, and, most importantly, that it will always arrive on time. But when satisfied about these criteria, many editors are only too glad to hand over responsibility for a portion of the paper and know they needn't worry about it any more.

Letting the editor know your worth by several times selling him other copy (and impressing him with your efficiency and dedication) is a good basis for asking for a regular column. (We'll refer to it as a 'column' even though it may be more or less.) On other occasions editors may invite you, out of the blue, but however it begins, a regular column is not something to be accepted lightly. Thinking you have a well of ideas that will never run dry is easy; tapping it day after day (or however frequently your column demands you do so) and finding it still full, or full enough, may be different. Fortuitously, I've found wells do have the magic property of being able to refill themselves; somehow, tapping the well of ideas gets the brain filling it up at increasing speed. I must not complain, therefore, because my own regular columns have gradually but inexorably imposed on me an instinctive habit of filling their particular wells even when I no longer want to tap them or at least want a break from doing so. Visiting friends, being on vacation, even when ill in hospital, I can't stop the wells filling. I do so much theatre reviewing that when I go to a show 'off duty', even before the interval my mind is turning round the intro, shape and viewpoint of review copy. I hope you can turn your brain off more satisfactorily than I can but if you are a slave to your head at least you will never run out of ideas.

Of equal importance is that your copy must never be late. *Never?* If you are whisked off for unexpected surgery or bereaved of a close family member nobody would expect you to keep up an uninterrupted supply. But relations coming to stay, taking your summer holiday, simply being too busy doing something else; try these as excuses for late copy and your editor won't keep you for long. The same rule applies for all copy, not just regular columns: short of real and rare emergencies, a *deadline must be kept*. The secret of being able to accept deadlines and still sleep at night may be this: plan ahead carefully, know your own writing capacity in terms of the research you may have to do for a particular item and the time it is likely to take you to write it, and (the best safety net in my opinion) have plenty of copy ready at home in your private store. Keep some ready to file, more half ready and only waiting for up-to-date material, and yet more awaiting your attention any time to maintain the quality and quantity of work in the store cupboard.

So what types of regular columns are out there waiting? Their themes are boundless: nature, profiles of famous people, chess, horoscopes, crosswords, competitions, children's and women's pages, young mothers, pop music, pets, food – anything that interests people will make a good column. You'll see I haven't mentioned travel or sport, motoring or business and finance. These are among the topics nearly always covered by staff writers (it's not hard to understand why) and contributions to these sections have to be exceptional, if not unique. Nevertheless, faint heart never won fair lady, despite well-established opposition, so don't fear to try your hand.

If the paper you choose doesn't already run a column on your topic you'll be in a better position than if you just contribute to one already run by somebody else. Regular columns can (and often do) involve you in other fascinating writing jobs. Mine have taken me on nationwide promotional tours, made me editor of annuals, given me more regular columns in other papers here and overseas as well as a lot of other work, and led to more pleasant surprises than I can recall. A column will get you known and your work constantly read and appreciated. There are pleasant byproducts too. Everybody wants you to include them or their pet/recipe/life story or whatever is relevant (and a heap of stuff that isn't!) and you should be ready for the feedback from readers. This can be one of the most rewarding aspects of column-running if you don't let it take up too much of your writing time. And what else? At the end of every month you are guaranteed a pre-negotiated regular fee without having to invoice anyone.

Reviews

The very special task of reviewing books, drama, films, videos, radio and television programmes is not work for a newcomer to writing. Someone famous in another sphere might be invited to review one book a week, a politician or a top sportsman, say, to attract readers with the name of the reviewer rather than his ability to review books but the quality papers have their own trained and experienced staff reviewers. How, then, do you gain experience? For all categories of reviewing it is only at the discretion of the editor (or features editor, for reviews usually come under his aegis) that you may be given a chance. If you've read this far you will know the only way to build up a solid reputation is to keep writing the copy he wants when (or preferably just before) he wants it; in other words by demonstrating your professionalism.

An editor is also wary of offering a reviewing job to an 'unknown' for fear of upsetting his staff who may be well-qualified to do it. Think too of the author, the playwright, the radio writer or the television scriptwriter who finds his work inadequately covered. A bad review by a professional reviewer is fair enough: a poorly written one by someone who doesn't know what he's doing is not. One of my worst recollections of theatre reviewing is finding myself sitting next to a young man covering for another paper who innocently confided to me that he had never before seen a stage show or even set foot in a theatre. Common politeness battled with horror as I almost sank through the seat. Pity the playwright, the producer, the cast and everyone else. Most of all, perhaps, pity the young man.

Fillers, anecdotes and humour

A filler is a small item, often just one or two sentences, used to fill up a little space in the paper. Writers may complain that because of the new technology and its advantage of easier page layout, there are fewer little spaces for fillers, but as in all marketing it is a matter of finding your own openings. Distinguish between news and general fillers as a newspaper may confine itself to one variety. I wouldn't recommend giving much of your time and trouble to these bits and pieces of writing but they do help to keep the mind ticking over in the right direction. Faced with a daily journey to and from a newspaper office I once promised myself it would provide at least two fillers a day, which it did quite easily. You could try the same; write them out later and file them to a paper when you've amassed a good collection... To a freelance writer nothing observed or overheard is ever wasted.

As a filler of the non-news type may be a mini-anecdote, so an anecdote on its own may be something to lighten a reader's heart, especially when it is combined with humour. Make 'em laugh and you'll have editors eating out of your hand. Whatever the seriousness of your chosen market readers will view it with greater affection if it – momentarily only, perhaps – makes them smile. One story I read concerned a woman whose family had been devastated by the loss of a baby who had died from a tragic childhood malfunction. The woman decided to help the support group for other babies suffering in the same way by collecting children's sayings and publishing them in a booklet to raise money. She put a request for anecdotes and stories in local papers and the laughs flooded in. This is my favourite:

> It was Christmas and the Junior School nativity play was at its most reverent point. But the live baby cast to bring realism to the leading role was bawling at the top of his voice, drowning the words of the Wise Men and attendant shepherds in their dressing gowns and threatening to ruin the whole production. The nine year old Virgin Mary tried to quieten him without success and at last could stand no more. Abandoning all much-practised saintliness she held the infant Messiah aloft, gave him a good shake and bellowed at the startled babe a line certainly never scripted in the New Testament: 'Gi' over, Jesus, will y'?'

Rows of parents and teachers fell about. Who can read that and not do the same?

It's important to note that in the story above the humour of the nativity play incident is not the main point, amusing though it is. Newspapers are not joke books or collections of funny stories. The humour only serves to bring to readers the deeper story underneath – in this case that a woman is raising money for a cause to touch all hearts – which itself provides a 'platform' for an anecdote readers will enjoy.

Having said that reminds me of a fellow writer who persuaded the editor of her evening paper that a 'funny' corner would give readers at least one thing to laugh at every day. That's her column now; it's been running for two years and the readers love it. A few other freelances specialise in writing humorous articles and pieces and obviously have a flair for doing so. It's easy to laugh at humour, not easy to write it and virtually impossible to teach someone how to do it. Lucky you if you know how.

4
How to Write It

Ready?

You've selected your subject, your special slant on it and what it's going to make (letter, feature, etc.) in which market, so you're ready to start writing. Or are you? One school of thought says, at this point, 'Write it down. You can always mess it about later, but until it's there in front of you – it's nothing.' That is not bad advice, but there can be a clinging permanency about those first efforts, particularly at the start of a writer's career when you may not yet possess the boldness to cut and prune what you've written. On the other hand, you may opt for not committing anything definite on paper for the moment, while you think over what your plan is and just how you are going to write it. Let's have a quick reappraisal of the preparation.

Your chosen market is – we'll imagine – the regional evening paper in your area and you want to write an article about the old cinema in a nearby town. Derelict for many years, the building is now being demolished but you feel it must have a fascinating past that shouldn't die without comment; your research has been thorough and you've discovered so much of interest to readers you are confident you have plenty of material.

This is a good place to remind ·you that stubborn determination to use every scrap of research material you have unearthed, relevant or not, can ruin a good feature. Don't feel you've been working to no purpose and wasting your time if you can't or don't use it all. In any case, you will (I hope) keep everything you've found. Its value in the future will more than reward you for any restraint this first article might impose on you. Never content yourself with writing just one or two pieces about a topic when your research will keep you funded to sell to local papers, freesheets, regional, trade and maybe daily papers, overseas, specialist and general magazines . . . and of course each article will be different from the others. I confess the only hardship I find in wringing research dry is that I get tired of the subject. I can be sure my readers won't, because they are never the same people reading the same thing.

You are equally optimistic about your first choice of market, the big evening paper in your area. You have delved back into the cinema's old days as a theatre and music hall and know that many old-time stars appeared there and had lodgings in the town at the time. You've dug deeper and found some of the families (or their offspring) where the 'stars' lodged, perhaps even some still living in the same houses. Some of the many people who worked in the old place in its heyday are delighted to share their recollections with you – and readers – and your research file is bulging with fascinating material.

This is just an example of the type of article you might be planning, but you could be envisaging something quite different. A report on your trek across South America, facts and figures about women's clubs, keeping your teeth in good condition, the incidence of broken marriages among servicemen and women overseas, the history of old coins unearthed in your area – no matter what your topic you will be wise to have done your homework before you start writing. Arrogantly, I nearly said 'you must have done your homework...' until I recalled a well-established writer friend who prefers to research a little to give himself the 'feel' of what he's doing, then write his piece, leaving little gaps where he knows he needs to do more research, and fill the gaps later. It works very well for him, and perhaps it would for you, although it isn't how I do it. It shows that in writing there is no inflexible rule about anything.

You've been in contact with the paper's features editor who has shown distinct interest in the subject and has asked to see what you have to offer – albeit without any firm commitment. He might have told you, if it is appropriate, that they will arrange pictures (unless you can do so yourself, to the required standard), and you know the length you will be writing to. You are quite familiar with the paper, reading it almost every evening, and in your mind's eye you can see your feature having a good spread, and – of course! – attracting lively and appreciative comment from nostalgic readers (with a good fee for you; have you discussed that with the paper?).

Then comes the moment you feel you are ready to write your rough draft. There's no need to start at the beginning for you can be happily uninhibited, as I know from much personal experience, because no eyes but yours will ever see your initial efforts. At this early stage you might take one or more sheets of rough A4 paper (the backs of other unwanted sheets) and sketch out a crude shape to the piece; a title, a strong intro (first par), a possible order of the main points of the article, a neat ending. Then what? Write it up? You could open with a bit of explanation about the story and why you're telling it, continue in a straightforward narrative about the history of the theatre and a more-or-less chronological progress through its fortunes and failures, and end with some regrets about its impending demolition. Will that suffice? NO! To follow that predictable recipe *with no other ingredients* might make it acceptable (if the editor were desperate or not feeling very well) but is also likely to make it ploddingly dull! The article – any article and every piece of writing of any sort – needs a lift, a buoyancy, what the advertising men call 'oomph' or 'zizz', to make it different and (most of all) irresistible. What it needs is style.

Style – for want of a better word

'That could be quite good,' was an editor's verdict on the writer's article in his hand. 'But it lacks style.' 'Thank you,' said the writer, adding, in some trepidation but in need of further enlightenment, 'What *is* style?' A little laugh was the only reply. It's not a question that expects an answer. So how is a freelance (or any other) writer to know what is 'good', what 'style' is, and how to acquire it? Consider this apparent paradox: your best style is what is naturally 'you': any accomplished writer can write in several styles. I believe the former statement applies at the start of one's writing career, the latter is certainly true with greater experience. Even then your style is 'you' as much as your voice, your mannerisms and the way you walk; it cannot be otherwise. You can adapt your writing style as you wish, although just now we are discussing style in the light of a definite market, a considered and researched topic, and the slant chosen for it. To a large degree these points will determine the writing style. But there is more to it than that.

There are writers who insist attempting to dissect style is to kill it and that if it does not come naturally, too bad; maybe you'll get better one day.

That's not my view. If I can reduce a problem into

manageable portions I improve my chances of getting to grips with it. Like readers of newspapers, I have a short attention span. For that reason I've narrowed down what I think 'style' means (although other writers may disagree with me, for perhaps style, like beauty, is in the eye of the beholder) and I here offer as simple a distillation of it as I can. With everything I write my hope is to let the following five factors loiter in the subconscious and trust they will weave some sort of spell. Occasionally they do: often they darn well won't. I list them here in no order of priority.

Clarity
The first factor is Clarity for if we don't make what we are trying to say crystal clear we might as well not bother to write it down. Try this:

> 'Anne met her mother at six o'clock. She had been working all day.'

Who had been working all day?

> 'Anne met her mother at six o'clock after working all day' makes it Anne; 'Anne met her mother at six o'clock and thought how tired she looked after working all day' makes it mother.

Here's another:

> 'The natives looked friendly but they didn't offer them any food.'

Who didn't offer any food and who didn't get any?

> 'The natives looked friendly but didn't offer the travellers any food' or 'The natives looked friendly but the travellers didn't offer them any food' clarifies who went hungry.

Accuracy
If Clarity begins at home, so does the second factor: Accuracy. This is not only getting facts right, important as that is, but also being accurate about how they sit on the page. Inaccuracy has two common causes, one of which is faulty sentence construction. I saw this in a national paper that ought to hang its head in shame:

> 'Standing on the bridge the National Theatre is an impressive sight.'

I can imagine a foreign tourist reading that and thinking, 'Wow, I must go and see that theatre built on a bridge!' I don't live in London but I do know the National Theatre does not stand on a bridge, so our foreign tourist friend is in for a disappointment. What the writer meant, of course, was:

> 'The National Theatre is an impressive sight seen from the bridge' or 'When you stand on the bridge…'.

Another newspaper item said:

> 'At the age of three her father took her to Canada.'

Advanced, wasn't he, for a three year old?

The other fault is using a word you think is the one you want when it isn't. 'Borrow' and 'lend' may be no problem but are you happy about 'infer' and 'imply', or 'principle' and 'principal', 'agoraphobia' and 'acrophobia'? What determines whether you use 'after' or 'afterwards'? I think it downright sneaky, by the way for 'invalid' to be the reverse of 'valid' but 'invaluable' not to be the reverse of 'valuable'.

What about 'fewer' and 'less'? (If you're wondering, 'fewer' can be counted but 'less' can't.) Are you a sucker for words like 'subliminal' (yes, I have a few favourites but they must know their place) or phrases such as 'expeditiously effected an exit' (left quickly)? Do you write redundant words: 'she filled up the kettle' instead of 'she filled the kettle', or 'there was more to follow later' instead of 'there was more to follow'? Are you guilty of 'different to' or 'fed up of'? Accuracy insists we must not write unthinkingly but here are three extracts culled in 1990 (International Literacy Year) from sources that might be expected to do better:

> 'The flower and float power in Jersey's annual Battle of Flowers is £240,000. And it really did used to be a fight.' (The ubiquitous PLUS magazine)

> 'A stroll through the Latin quarter of Paris on a Saturday night would not be the same without seeing the squads sat in their heavily barred Renault buses.' (The Sunday Telegraph, no less)

> 'He goes on to ask if, having entered poems for competitions which were subsequently published in an anthology, it would affect his being able to have them published at a later date in another volume of poems?' (a writers' magazine)

Listen to people talking and you will often hear words used

incorrectly; we are all guilty at times. 'Hopefully' is one that may alter the interpretation of a sentence, often without the speaker being aware of it. 'The bypass will be completed next year' is a bald statement. 'Hopefully the bypass will be completed next year' immediately reveals a personal view. People living in houses bordering the bypass might not agree; 'regrettably' could reflect their feelings more adequately. This objection apart, 'hopefully' is an adverb – a word added to a verb to express a modification of it. Is a bypass capable of hope, or regret? Following the current trend in talking is not necessarily the best way to write for papers of any level. We don't want to talk like textbooks on English grammar and speech has a brief life. But put any solecism, however minor, in writing and you bestow on it a credibility it doesn't deserve.

In appreciating the need for keeping abreast of how people think, how are your cliches? Remember they suffer from terminal illnesses! Phrases and sayings are sharp and appropriate the first time round, not so endearing when you've heard them a few times and a screaming bore when you find them at every turn. So today's cliches may be tomorrow's groans. There's nothing new under the sun? Perhaps, for I thought 'In this office, cliches will be avoided like the plague' very clever when I saw it on the wall of a newspaper office. People around me sighed; I should at least have noticed the cutting was going brown at the edges. Stereotyped writing is another hazard. Do you use phrases that should have lain down and died years ago? (Are you happy that 'lain' is the right word here, or do you suspect it should be 'laid'?)

Newspapers like adjectives only when they have something to say. They should inform or describe but never make the reader stop with a query. 'Long' doesn't tell him how long; 'short' is how short? And there are pairs of words that are not interchangeable although most of us are not sure which to use where. Like these:

'The cake that my mother baked for me was delicious.'
'The cake which my mother baked for me was delicious.'

Which is correct? Hands up who chose the second? Good. The reasoning behind the distinction is this: 'that' defines and 'which' informs. This is an over-simplification, of course, for the sake of clarity and both sentences would be better without 'that' or 'which' at all. The point is that in the first sentence 'that' assumes readers already know my mother baked the cake and I am simply referring to it again so they will know which particular cake I'm talking about. In the second sentence 'which' introduces new information about the cake, regardless of whether readers have heard about it before or not. As for any commas there might or might not be in these sentences – read on.

I've mentioned the matter of 'he or she', 'him or her', and so on at the start of this book but it constantly crops up as a thorn in newspaper copy. What do you think of this?

'I like Wensleydale cheese. But everyone to his or her favourite.'

Ugh! Does anybody like the taste of that? Melting down the cheese is the only solution. Using plurals is one way of recasting the sentence: 'People have their favourites'. Chickening out of 'his or her' is another: 'Everyone has a favourite'. 'We all have our favourites' is a third and the one I would choose, partly because it flows more easily in print but chiefly because the 'we' puts me on the same level as the reader, and everything I write should be viewed through his eyes and not mine. Using the first person plural gives this 'one of us' feeling quite naturally. Contrast such usage with 'It is thought' or 'It is said' (by whom, anyway?) which is totally impersonal. In quality papers in the right circumstances, fine; in lighter vein it drives a ditch between you and your readers – and why should they bother to jump over it?

Euphony
Third on my list is Euphony. Be it a news story, an article, just a Letter to the Editor or even a filler, euphony is something you only notice when it isn't there. A piece of written work may be silent words on paper but take them all together and there is – or should be – a rhythm, a satisfaction, a *something* that helps the reader feel at the end, 'Yes, that was well written'. You think this is pretentious talk that would be scorned by your local paper or freesheet? Not at all. As children learning to read we hear the words in our heads although we may not say them aloud, but with maturity comes that curious state of absorbing what we read without being aware of it; we no longer read individual words strung together, but whole pieces of written work. Indeed, so strong is this 'absorption' concept it is almost impossible *not* to use it; showing cards to prisoners for two seconds, announcing their

imminent execution, in a language they deny knowledg considered a sophisticated and effective form of tortu. some repressive regimes.

We writers refer to the 'flow of writing' or 'being in full flow' and perhaps when that is happening the euphony factor is taking over subconsciously, exactly as we want it to. It's easy to spoil it, to 'lose the flow', as we all know. Ambiguity, a muddled phrase, getting facts wrong, chasing up a blind alley and then trying to slide out of trouble – all these can break the euphony. So can a sudden unwarranted switch in viewpoint or tense, a misplaced fact, or inconsistency in mood. In practical terms inadequate attention to structure, paragraph size and punctuation can jar readers out of sympathy in a trice. When that happens they instantly lose their 'absorption' capacity and find themselves floundering amidst individual words. Euphony gives way to exasperation. 'What he means is…' they frown, or 'That bit ought to read….'

We tend to talk in longer sentences than we use in writing, because speaking is so much more rapid. It can be a surprise to count the number of words most newspapers use 'in one breath'. Seven or eight is not abnormal for a sentence in the tabloids, especially that important opening sentence. For a proper assessment and to satisfy your market's requirements it is worth studying a paper's density. This is a practical formula for working out how easy or difficult it is to read and understand. It's done by taking the number of words in an average sentence and comparing it to the average number in a piece of your normal writing (when you're not making a special effort to conform to any particular style). Fifteen or 16 is considered intellectually suitable for readers at university level, and 12 or 13 for the average school leaver.

Work it out like this: from the paper take any extract of 100 words (give or take one or two) finishing at the end of a sentence. Count the number of sentences in that extract and divide 100 by that number. This gives you the average length of the sentences in the extract. Now count the number of words of more than two syllables and add that figure to the average sentence length. Halve the result and you have the paper's density. Here is an example:

Number of sentences in extract	=	10
100 divided by 10	=	10 = average sentence length.
Words of more than 2 syllables	=	22
10 + 22	=	32
Half 32	=	16 = paper's density.

Because the number of words of more than two syllables is part of the formula for establishing the density of a paper, the result will also indicate the simplicity or difficulty of its words compared to other papers. Now try it with any extract of your own work. Your density is higher? Come 'down' a bit. But if yours is less than the paper you've chosen maybe you should be making a more up-market choice.

To establish and maintain euphony vary sentence length, even within the paper's density. And don't forget sentences of one or two words or without verbs have a valid place: we are talking to people in their own language, not writing a postgraduate thesis. Variety of construction is important, too, lest we drone and bore. An adjectival phrase, for instance, can be a useful opener for the occasional sentence but is an irritant if used to excess. Here's an overdose:

> 'Wanting to catch the train, Jack rushed across to his car. Trusting traffic would be light that morning... Thinking the office might be closed and fearing he would be too late... Worried he might not have another chance....'

Could you bear much more of that?

Alliteration has its place but the pages of newspapers may not be where you'll find much of it, except, perhaps, in feature material – and then sparingly. It's a question of common sense and – like so much in this book – being made aware of pitfalls so you can avoid falling into them. All this about euphony and style shouldn't blind us to a matter of fact: to write for a newspaper you may have your head filled with ambition for the quality of what you write (indeed you must have that ambition) but there's only one place for your feet at all times: on the ground.

Brevity

We're up to factor four which is Brevity. It's so important I would have placed it higher had I been establishing an order of importance. Brevity doesn't mean, as I thought in my youth, cut and cut and cut until only the bare bones of a piece remain (sometimes there was nothing left by the time I'd finished). Nor, of course, is it only writing short pieces ('Oh good,' think the ingenuous, 'that's easy.'). Brevity means telling in 200 words a story you've first written in 400, *leaving out nothing that matters*. Call it conciseness or economy instead, if you prefer; it is the essence of good writing and a skill learned by constant observation and practice. See how you score by writing a piece and then re-writing it more tightly, or by trying to improve on what someone else has written, always remembering the criterion of not cutting out anything important.

As an aid to brevity I recommend making sure a high proportion of your writing sticks firmly to the point. Rough judgement about how well it does this is hardly enough as you skim through the completed draft. Count the words that truly relate to the topic; the number will depend on what it is and your slant on it, but the higher the proportion of relevant words and phrases the tighter your copy will be.

Train yourself to start at the beginning. This is not as foolish as it may sound, for beginners often meander round the edge of a story before getting to its nuts and bolts. That first sentence bears a heavy burden! Look at yours. Is it about the story you are just going to unfold, explaining how you come to be writing it, perhaps, or why it is such a tricky subject to write about? If it is, delete it. A fair test is to put the story aside for a few days so you can come to it with a sharper critical sense and then start reading it from the third or even the fourth paragraph. If you realise that is where the story really begins, cut out those waffly ones that came first.

Death to all wimps! Eliminating them is another way to tighter writing. Words and phrases that don't work for a living are wimps and have no place in newspaper copy. Spot the wimps in this:

'The villages are quite large and a good number of the people live by fishing and a spot of hunting. Their huts are very small and very overcrowded, especially when three or more generations manage to live together under one roof.'

Hmm. Awful, isn't it? More wimps here than holes in a net. 'Quite large' and 'very small' mean nothing without a yardstick. Is a cat quite large to a mouse or an elephant? Are beans very small compared to apples or grains of rice? How many people is 'a good number'? And what about a 'spot of hunting'? That sounds more like a jolly day's sport up at the manor, don't you know, than a (presumably) practical food-gathering method of people living in huts. 'Very' is back for the overcrowding and I can't think how people of any age ranges could live together and not be 'under one roof'. Incidentally, I copied the piece from a report in a regional evening paper. Slapped wrists for whoever wrote it; I hope the editor's recovered his senses by now.

Writing with brevity is nothing more than stepping back, taking a hard look at what you've written and being ruthless when you need to be. Long-windedness, repetition without cause, talking off the subject, vagueness, dragging and not knowing where the article is going are slicing points. Be brave! (You'll save yourself time, of course, if you learn to write with brevity in the first place.)

Magic

Writing for newspapers is, as I repeatedly stress, practical and functional. There is little room for what is commonly termed the 'art' of writing, although in my view the business of writing what is wanted clearly and simply is itself an art. Despite this no-nonsense approach, the best newspaper writers manage – at the right moment, according to what they're writing – to lift readers above the story, to give them a sudden glow or to lighten what might be a black period in their lives. It is done in several ways, and if these include carefully selected artifice the effect is no less heart-warming. Writing of every sort is partly artifice, when all's said and done, or we're back to the folk who imagine that if it doesn't come entirely naturally you're not a writer. (We all know the futility of barking up that tree; these folk must believe learning is wrong.) Artifice has a poor reputation because it sounds deceitful and 'on the make', but I use it here only with readers' best interests in mind. I believe artifice is only permissible when used with depth and honesty. Figures of speech and emotive words with special impact can make a happy incident linger in a reader's memory where bald narrative might not; touching a nostalgic or deeply-buried chord may raise a childlike wonder and optimism not experienced for years. If they are relevant to a story, your own emotions, not in sickly sentimentality nor tongue-in-cheek and certainly never in excess, can let readers know somebody cares, they're not alone in their troubles, or there truly is light at the end of their particular tunnel. The 'magic' factor can draw from readers that contented sigh we all want to hear, 'Ah, that's good'.

That's what I call style.

House style

A newspaper's 'house style' is very different from the style we've been talking about above. Observing the house style means following established rules and customs in punctuation, paragraphing, the use of capital letters and hyphens, the precise way of writing numbers, dates, abbreviations and everything else that has to be set in text. The rules exist only for the convenience of everyone writing for the paper (no more of that uncertainty about whether to give them '1, 2, 3' or 'one, two, three' and so on) and for consistency. It would look ill-organised to print 'Doctor F Higgins Jones' in one par and refer to him lower down the page as 'Dr. F. Jones', or to print 'etcetera' on page 2 and 'etc.' on page 4. The latter raises a typical 'house style' problem: 'etcetera' is, I think, unique in being spoken in full but commonly written in abbreviated form. In its shortened form, does 'etc' have a full stop after it when it's in the middle of a sentence, only at the end of a sentence, in both situations or in neither? The house style will supply the answer.

It is not just a fetish of the editor or someone on high, for inconsistencies can leap off printed pages and detract from the story. Pointing out such irregularities was a favourite topic for Letters to the Editor before the introduction of house style books. Nowadays they tend to lie around offices getting dirty and lost; if you can't get hold of one (and a request may be treated with bemused astonishment) I suggest you make your own by keeping an eye on the newspaper of your choice and making a note of any quirkiness that may have you falling over.

Scaffolding and building

Perhaps all we need to know is that if the reader has to adjust his interpretation of what he's reading half way through (and go back and start again, if he's sufficiently interested) there's something mighty wrong with it. Capricious scaffolding could be the weakness. The worst weakness in building anything is to let the scaffolding show when the piece is completed. The designer knows it was there, it was the only structure that held the whole edifice together at the beginning, and nothing could have been built at all without it. A writer is the designer and the builder, but first he has to erect the scaffolding. It must be strong.

Broadly speaking, a piece of work other than the briefest is shaped into paragraphs. They are not chunks of prose cut at random, for paragraphing has a definite purpose. It breaks up copy to make it more attractive to read; a large slab of print is a deterrent to the casual reader and if he skips past your article without sampling it he won't know if he even likes the taste. A paragraph talks about one aspect of your main topic (just as a sentence has a single thought) and when you've finished with that aspect it is time to move on to the next par with the next point you wish to make. What do you do if what you want to say is going to take a lot of space, making it too long a par for comfort? Why, break it up into two or more! There's no rule that says you must contain all you want to say at that moment in a single par. It is more important not to deter a reader with an indigestible block of words. As with sentences, varying the length of paragraphs makes for a lighter and more easily swallowed article.

Variety in paragraph construction is also important in making the written piece easy on the eye and effortlessly taken into the head. The first par or 'intro' of any piece has a particular job: to keep people reading. People don't read papers in the same way as they might read fiction. They could be reading newspapers while standing at bus stops or taking a quick tea break and the story in front of them cannot afford a leisurely beginning. Intros, therefore, must hit the nail straight on the head, besides being simple and capable of being absorbed at once. I find my best ones when I'm not sitting at my desk. Maybe I'm driving, or in the bath; being denied the help of a scribbling pad forces me to an intro that is vivid and brief – or I'll forget it before I can write it down. When I do, it often says just what I want it to say.

As we saw above in the case of adjectival phrases starting too many sentences, the involuntary repetition of a particular 'shape' can make one par look like another, regardless of its content. Read a couple of pages of a feature in a quality daily or regional paper and notice how adopting a different strategy for each par avoids giving readers the same doorstep to climb over and over again.

The topic and slant will determine the tenor of the pars you write and a news story, for example, will be written more crisply than a feature. Whatever form of writing it is, does narration tell the story effectively or is exposition more appropriate? The active voice (being more positive and immediate) is usually better in news stories than the passive, but all paragraphs, as indeed, all sentences and even all words, must keep the story moving along. Being specific is better than being general and plain words are often best.

'Said' and 'began' are easier on the inward ear than 'responded' and 'commenced'. 'Died' has a starkness lacked by 'came to the end of his life'.

If you find it hard to identify different paragraph shapes, listen to the radio and imagine you have to present in written form a report about – say – whaling in Alaska. As you listen, think where you would end one par and open a new one. And here's another tip.

To build the written piece one paragraph has to follow its predecessor smoothly; it needs a 'joiner'. Two sentences before this one you've had one of the best! Puzzled? Let me explain.

A newspaper writer knows he must keep readers reading and that means keeping them sufficiently interested to bridge the mental jump of eye and brain from one par to the next. That's hardly a difficult jump, you could be thinking. But drifting to another item on the page is sometimes easier. So we use a technique to keep them reading, by leaving a little 'come-on' dangling at the end of a paragraph. Go back a couple of pars to one we'll call par A. It ends with a short sentence 'And here's another tip'. This is a come-on to entice you into reading par B (although this device is less appropriate in books and I use it here merely to illustrate a technique). Look more closely and you'll see another come-on at the end of that short par B in 'Let me explain'. A good public speaker will use the same technique before pausing to take a sip of water, to deter folk in the audience from using the break to make a bolt for the exit.

Paragraph joiners may be phrases or single words and you can spot them at the start of many a good par. Out of place, they can make your pars overdressed; 'moreover', 'nevertheless', and 'notwithstanding' make the less portentous 'however' more acceptable, but even that is hardly the normal parlance of tabloid readers. 'All the same' and 'even so' are more comfortable, but – as always – the market is boss. 'Yet', 'but', 'despite', and conjunctions of time like 'when' come naturally. And there's nothing amiss about joining with 'and', hesitant as you might be to make your old schoolteacher flinch.

Many joiners serve more than the purpose of linking one par to the previous one. As 'and' continues with what you're saying, 'for' introduces a reason, a result, or a new development, 'so' is tantamount to saying 'and the consequence is, or was' and 'but' involves a stepping back and looking at the matter from the other side. 'Now' can be patronising and should be used with care. It may be a complacent pause by a writer more fascinated by what he's writing than is good for him; usually what it says is 'at last we're getting to the point of this story'.

'I love punctuation', says a colleague of mine. 'Semi-colons where others fear to tread, commas like confetti at a wedding, points (full-stops) put a halt to any nonsense, and many an exclamation mark's saved a glass being thrown when I'm outraged or exasperated. Wonderful stuff.'

It must be the ease with which punctuation is sprinkled about that makes it so tempting but it is best used with restraint. Its *raison d'être* is two-fold: to facilitate smooth reading and to ensure what has been written is not misunderstood. In its latter capacity it guards against ambiguity. If you don't know your colon from your inverted commas your punctuation could be doing quite the reverse. (I hope the confusion that would and sometimes does occur when folk who consider grammar and punctuation beneath them have their way is enough to convince wavering readers of its importance.) We need to know the function of the different punctuation marks and where they should be placed. That means observing the rules of basic grammar, which is no more than acquiring the ability to write English we could show our grandmothers without a blush.

If you're in need of a brush up on what you learned at school or can't remember learning, get hold of a guide to English grammar by a well-qualified tutor (see Chapter 6) and take careful note of how quality papers use punctuation. The latter, by the way, will help you absorb the house style – and for the moment we'll ignore those awful errors that sometimes creep into print.

You may not elicit all you need to know from newspapers. Consider this:

> 'The boys, who arrived too late, found all the tickets had been sold.'

Both those commas should be omitted. A comma works hard in its role of providing a breathing space for the reader but this sentence is short enough not to need one. Note the difference between a subsidiary clause that *defines* (contributing information of substance) and one that *describes* (merely adding information). Not sure which is which? If it can be left out without hurting the sentence it's descriptive. There are instances where this test doesn't apply, but they are rare. The point to remember is that defining clauses hate being fenced off between commas. In the sentence quoted above 'who arrived too late' is plainly definitive as it explains why they didn't get any tickets. More subtly, sandwiching 'who arrived too late' between commas relegates that snippet of information to markedly less significance than what you imply is to follow. As that is not the case here, the reader is left with a whiff of dissatisfaction.

Changing the sentence to 'The boys, who were wearing green shirts, found...' makes the subsidiary clause descriptive; it adds information by telling us the colour of the boys' shirts. Apply the test. The commas should be left in place. You disagree? Cut them out, then, and we're left with 'The boys who were wearing green shirts found all the tickets had been sold'. Ah, readers not party to this discussion might think, so boys in red or yellow or blue shirts got tickets but the organisers refused to sell any to green shirt-wearers. No, that's not what we mean, is it? There must be something in this punctuation business after all; it's not just pedantic nonsense.

Alas, writing good English and punctuating it well is one thing but writing for newspapers can be rather different. Only you can decide which markets to write for and the work you do. Should you ever feel disheartened about standards remember there are papers to satisfy everybody, and no matter which you choose, you must put yourself in the place of their readers if you wish to sell your work.

There are countless tricks of the trade professional journalists use every day: implying something without actually saying it, repetition for a particular reason, slowing up or quickening pace, deliberate facetiousness, compression for a special effect. All these techniques give impact and colour. Read papers with a 'new' eye and you can't help but learn more.

At last your piece is done – almost. How do you end it? This is called 'casting-off'. Its prime demand is urgency; when you've finished, *finish*. If you meander on with extra thoughts you should have inserted earlier or ones that don't belong in the story, a sub-editor will cast-off for you. Then it may not be a cast-off so much as a cut-off, which is usually as unsatisfactory an experience as is its verbal cousin on the telephone.

Casting-off simply means ending the story succinctly and at

the right time – which is what the writer should do. Cutting-off is what the sub-editor does when the copy overruns. It is either too long for the space allotted for it or, more probably, it doesn't end at the end of the story. Woe to the writer whose work is cut-off! If he has saved his *pièce de résistance* till last it's likely to suffer a *coup de grâce*. It's not a scrap of good complaining. He has nobody to blame but himself.

News stories

There's an old saying in newspaper offices: 'When you've heard half a dozen eye-witnesses describe what happened at the scene of an accident, you begin to wonder about history.' Plainly what is a fact to me may not always be the same to you, and yours may not tally with the one the man next door insists is right. How do we straighten out this conundrum?

The world is round (more or less) and I am my mother's daughter. These are facts. But report a news story and what you'll be listening to at any one time is one person's opinion, although the speaker is convinced what he is saying is 'fact'. He's not lying (probably) but he may still be wrong; what he's telling you may not be fact at all. That is just one reason why news stories are tricky to write. It is important to seek 'facts' from as many people on the scene as you can.

There's another reason why a news story needs to be written with special care; we're back to the cutting-off, which can inflict a mortal wound. The accepted method is to make it a pyramid. Let us say we have a story about a twelve year old boy who was taken to a local maternity home to have his tonsils out; a 'fun' story to write and one offering plenty of scope in a jokey style.

If we were telling this innocuous tale to a friend we would enjoy building it up and keeping the punch line – the boy's destination – to the end. Isn't that how all the best funny stories go? Try that format as a newspaper piece and the end may never be printed at all. Being too long is the usual reason for a cut-off, but it may not always be the writer's fault. There might be a change in the page layout for all sorts of reasons, and no way can the freelance writer anticipate a shortage of space for news. The safeguard, therefore, is to write a news story so that if anything's going to be cut, it will only be 'small' subsidiary matter at the end of it. Like this:

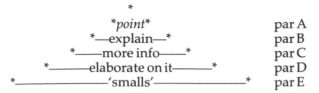

```
              *
         *point*                    par A
      *—explain—*                   par B
    *——more info——*                 par C
  *——elaborate on it——*             par D
*——————'smalls'——————*             par E
```

Remember those good old questions every journalist should ask on a news story? The pyramid uses them all. I like Rudyard Kipling's version:

'I kept six honest serving men,
They taught me all I knew,
Their names are WHAT and WHY and WHEN,
And HOW and WHERE and WHO.'

You need to watch the length of each par as well (or you may defeat the whole purpose) but in shape and substance the story will follow the pyramid above. Paragraph A will be the nub of it, the point that makes it news.

'Twelve year old Matthew Smith thought he knew the facts of life until he had his tonsils out in a maternity home...' (continue as you wish, with the answers to the questions 'Who?' and 'What?').

Par B allows you space to explain what you've already written in par A, this time having discovered more in answer, perhaps, to the questions 'Where?' 'When?' and 'Why?'. But par B should not exceed par A in significance.

Down to par C and room for further information, but only matters of less importance to the story as a whole. Then to par D and here may come details that wouldn't be missed, perhaps answering the question 'How?'

Lastly comes poor par E, the fall-guy. It should only carry the 'smalls', i.e. extra little bits you might still wish to use, but which don't contribute to the news value of the story. That being so, should par E be there at all? Don't use 'smalls' as an excuse to overwrite the story. An editor or sub-editor might not cut it; he might find it less trouble to spike it and not use it at all.

Letters to the editor

Most newspapers print a letters column, or even a full page of them. This is a part of the paper that is widely-read because it tends to reflect everyday issues of immediate interest to most of the paper's readers. You may think this type of writing is a waste of your efforts if you won't get paid for it, but think again. It is generally understood that some papers do not pay (although others do) but contributions to the letters page are always worth a writer's time and effort. They can be mulled over in your head at any odd moments, take only a few moments to jot down and not many more to lick into shape.

A good Letter to the Editor can persuade him to do something or take a special interest in some event, or it may initiate news coverage of the points raised in it. Letters may reflect genuine wishes, nostalgia, observations, indignation, complaints and (less frequently) praise from the paper's ordinary readers.

Many letters never see the dark of print. Excessive moaning and negative criticism are first in the waste paper basket, although constructive argument on a topic already raised can make good reading. 'I can't agree with…' is quite welcome if followed by an addition to something already written about, or bringing a new perspective to it. The height of your neighbour's sunflowers, why buses don't run on time in your area, a useful tip for mothers with young babies in cold weather, your favourite recipe for lemon curd jam, why you fear for Anglo-Chinese relations in the light of current events or why a remand home should not be built near your town; controversy may be a successful ingredient, brevity *always* is and almost every topic from almost every viewpoint is your stock in trade. But letters are not always as innocuous or spontaneous as they may seem to be.

One colleague of mine (I'll call him John) uses them like this: he remembers it is, for example, the anniversary of the date when a past monarch granted the freedom of the city to a tireless lady charity worker who is now in an old people's home. The granting of such freedoms is noteworthy, but John has made a study of them and has an article drafted on just this topic, with special reference to the honour it brought the city umpteen years ago; he also has some pictures of the old lady, with cuttings from the city's evening paper at that time, celebrating the event. Were John to submit his article to the editor 'cold' it could well be ignored among the many current events the paper has to cover. But, he tells me, any good gardener prepares his soil to give his plants a better chance of blooming.

Before the anniversary John has in mind a letter will arrive on the editor's desk. It shows a reader's pride in his city, and reminds the editor of the royal visit in such-and-such a year. Apart from the facts it reveals, there will be two essential points about this letter: it will be sent at exactly the right time (dictated by the frequency of publication) and it will not be written by John. The timing must be precise so the editor may be sufficiently interested to start looking round for a feature on the subject, and as for the letter writer – John has many friends and relations the other side of the city.

Dishonest, you say? He would laugh at such naïveté, vowing many a writer uses this way of arousing local interest, which is no more than people do when placing advertisements about forthcoming events. But there could be a snag. If John doesn't get his article to the editor at the right time, other readers may take up the topic and flood the editor with letters about it. Those words 'This correspondence is now closed' may kill off the goose for the very writer who laid the golden egg. Also, it could be that another writer (you?) (without any of John's guile) have spotted in the Letters to the Editor a 'peg' for an article you have ready to submit. Quite innocently, your enterprise may spoil John's little plan.

All Letters to the Editor should be brief and to the point, making it at the beginning rather than the middle or end. It is all too easy for a sub-editor to be interrupted by someone calling, the telephone ringing or by some other small distraction – and truncate your precious thoughts. Make each letter about just one point, and with perhaps fewer than fifty words to play with you need to get to it straight away.

It's not hard to see which of the following would stand the better chance of publication. This:

> 'I like to see dogs running about by the river just as they did when I was a youngster, because it reminds me of a neighbour's old collie we often used to play with, me and my friends. It was a gentle dog, I remember, and really wouldn't hurt a fly, except that one day....'

Or this:

> 'A dog pulled me out of a river when I was five, so I can't criticise owners....'

Use casual language, as if you are talking to a friend. Split your infinitives if you feel like it, and write 'won't' and 'can't' rather than 'will not' and 'cannot' if it sounds natural to do so.

Letters columns or pages often get 'put to bed' early in the life of the paper to get them out of the way and let the staff's attention be given to more topical matters. It pays (if not literally) to see yours arrive on the Editor's desk the first time he sits down to start assembling his next issue. For a weekly this will usually be the day after publication of the previous issue. Daily and evening papers naturally attract more letters, so although your chances of publication may seem higher, the reverse may be the case and it can be harder to aim your letter to a particular day or date. You can only hope for the best by writing a letter the editor simply cannot ignore, despite the large pile already claiming his attention.

A word of warning: getting your letter published is fine; coping with some of the repercussions of its publication may not be so agreeable. A lot of letters go without comment, except perhaps from your admiring family and friends, but if you have invited readers of the paper to respond to something (finding an old friend you've lost touch with, perhaps, supplying a recipe for loganberry wine or telling you where to buy clogs) don't be surprised if they do just what you've asked – in great numbers. You should be ready to reply to everybody who writes to you, and this can take more time and trouble than you bargained for!

Although Letters to the Editor are an important and valued part of the paper, it's not wise to telephone asking if they're going to print yours and if so please will they send you a free copy, or saying that you only want to know so you can tell all your friends to rush out and buy the paper. Don't fear, either, that you will be barred because you have had letters published in the same pages on other occasions; some writers become real 'characters' whose opinions evoke more from others and are read with affection or scorn or amusement, so their latest contributions will be received with special pleasure. Avid writers cover many topics and just keep writing; *The Guardian* has a few now regarded as old friends, especially one who writes to the Letters page two or three times a week. He doesn't mind that not all his letters are published, as he only spends a few minutes on each. So don't pester. It isn't that the editor doesn't care about you or that he doesn't welcome your letter, merely that – frankly – he also has larger matters to work on.

Typed letters are preferred although this is the one part of the paper where handwritten copy is acceptable; letters, after all, are invited from everyone – and not everyone is expected to own or have access to a typewriter, let alone a word-processor. Nor is it necessary to send a stamped-addressed envelope; you will be wasting money if you do for no letters are returned, even those that are not published. You have bought the paper, goes the thought, so you are entitled to give the editor your views, just as he has the right to publish or ignore them.

Writing Letters to the Editor may fill odd moments or keep you writing in an otherwise blank spell. It can provide agreeable satisfaction when you turn to the 'Letters' page in the paper, and may put a few pounds in your pocket; it's certainly not to be sneezed at.

What's more, have your letters published in newspapers and you'll be in the distinguished company of George Bernard Shaw, Arthur Conan Doyle, Graham Greene, Evelyn Waugh and Kingsley Amis, among other well-known writers, not forgetting Disgusted of Tunbridge Wells.

5
Interviews

Open any newspaper and you are bound to find at least one interview. A politician concerned in a current issue, the latest sporting champion, the author of a recent bestseller, a leading pop star, someone in the news or with an unusual story to tell – these are the kind of people readers want to know about. Whoever the interviewees are and whatever they have to say, you can be sure they would not be featured if that last point were not true. That's the major criterion, after all, and mere topicality is not enough. Will the paper's readers be interested?

'Who shall it be?'

Planning to interview someone needs as careful market study as does writing of any other type. I make particular mention of this because interviewing is a craft in many respects apart from most other work done by freelance writers. And the first question to answer is: 'Who will be the subject, a good person to interview?'

Choose wisely. It is not always a good idea to let our own preferences dictate to us. Many suitable people will not be well-known in more than their immediate area, whereas an achievement of special interest or a personal story from an unknown person could make ideal material. In the first case the attraction will be the interviewee; in the second it will be his story. Either or both could be valid reasons for your choice.

As the primary reason for interviewing anybody is his topicality value to potential readers, the famous and the not so famous must pass the same test. Are they of interest to enough of the paper's readers for the editor to accept your idea? If you have the chance to interview a leading person in any field, you'll find most editors will be delighted; suggest a 'top' interviewee and you could even be selling your proposition to the highest bidder!

When you propose an interview with Mr Z to an editor there could be several explanations if he's not impressed. Newspaper spies are everywhere and he may know (as you do not) that a rival paper already has Mr Z lined up for an early issue. Mr Z may not merit the publicity the paper needs for a particular sales target. There could already be an interview with him in the pipeline. He may have a reputation, as yet unknown to you, of being more trouble than he is worth, demanding retractions, fees, apologies and so on.

But when all bodes well and the interviewee is just right for the paper, an editor will be even more pleased if he can arrange prior publicity. Circulation, revenue and the paper's image will receive a welcome boost. This is one reason why most interviews are commissioned pieces. The initial idea may come from you or the editor, and if he is confident of your ability there should be no trouble in fixing a definite commission for the job. 'Confident of your ability' sounds awesome, and that's just what interviewing can be if you plunge into it with insufficient thought. How long is the interview to be? Will there be accompanying pix taking some of 'your' space? Does the editor ask for a particular type of interview, or is it assumed you know the market and how to write for it?

Incidentally, after a little practice you'll find newspaper interviewing more like *fun* than work. You meet so many fascinating people (even if you don't actually like them all!) and, for a little time at least, enter a world that may be very different from your own, and which you might otherwise have no opportunity of sampling. Above all, as long as the world is full of people you'll never run out of raw material.

Fixing it up: time and place

Just when to approach your interviewee for consent to the project will be determined by circumstances. You may have enough time to make the agreement first, with date, hour and place all arranged, and then begin your preparatory work; or you might consider your interviewee will decline unless you can show some evidence of having done at least some of your homework at the first approach; only you can choose the most auspicious time to make it. Whatever you decide, remember some folk will be scared by the very word 'interview' but could respond favourably if you were to ask if they would like to 'talk' to you for the paper. Explain who you are, which paper will be publishing your interview (or you hope will be publishing it, if you are not yet commissioned), why you want to talk to him, about what, and indicate that you will readily fit in with his plans concerning dates, times, the length of the interview and so on.

What if your potential interviewee declines? Only you can decide whether a refusal means he's just playing hard to get and will give in if you're more persistent, or that he's learned to be wary of newspaper journalists (yes, when a few behave despicably, as they do, we all have to suffer) or he genuinely does *not* want any publicity. In this tough and uncompromising world of newspapers some journalists will urge you to be ruthless, to ignore pleas for privacy and to hit hard if you want to succeed, regardless of other people's wishes. I can't.

It is important to opt for the 'best' time and place for the interview (if you are in a position to choose) for both frequently affect the result. An interview over a meal is not to be recommended unless you are skilled at balancing plates with pens and notebooks, eating, drinking, asking questions and recording the answers all at the same time. Accommodating the interviewee's wishes is kindly and could make him feel well disposed towards you, but try to make sure the meeting is somewhere not likely to be disrupted by outside influences.

Written consent is seldom necessary. If he's a person in the public eye his secretary or manager will have a note of it, although you may like to confirm your part of the agreement in writing to ensure there are no mistakes regarding place, time, length of interview, likes and dislikes about tape recorders, and so on. The less well-known sometimes like to help with research, in the interests of their own publicity. This is quite acceptable as long as there is no onus on you to feature any particular aspect of their lives or work. The shape and plan of the interview is in *your* hands; let's hope it does not become necessary to remind your interviewee of this fact!

Preparation

The business of interviewing is in three parts: preparation, taking the interview, and writing it up afterwards. Preparation is like an iceberg in that nine-tenths will be hidden. It is often helpful to let a tenth show, for when you first approach your interviewee he will probably feel flattered on realising you have taken the trouble to do at least some 'outline' homework about him. Later, during the course of the interview itself, the time and effort you have invested in preparation will prove its worth. So don't skimp on this part of the job part; it may involve the most work but the more thoroughly it is done, the easier – and more pleasant – will be the interview that follows.

It is essential to familiarise yourself with your 'victim' so you don't waste time at the interview asking him questions you could well have found answers to before you met. Unbeknown to him, therefore, you will be delving into his past. The more you find out about him, his background, family, career, likes, dislikes and anything else you can discover, the greater your confidence will be when you meet him face to face.

The way to find help for every sort of project is fully discussed in the next chapter, and when planning an interview you will also be able to use research material uniquely relevant to your interviewee. His friends working in his field of expertise, for example, with the same hobbies or shared experiences, may be able to give you information not to be found in any book. At the very least they will guide you on the vocabulary and basic knowledge of his special subject or achievement; without some grasp of what he may talk about you could soon get confused.

Cuttings already published about him will be valuable and may include previous interviews containing useful information. Perhaps he refers to a favourite sport or leisure occupation, or personal details may be revealed. Press releases may be available. Gather all information in your private notes, regardless, at this stage, of how you might or might not make use of it. (Later, when you are more experienced in interviewing skills, you may have enough confidence to tackle the problem of selection as you do your research but I do not advise such early restriction before you feel happy about it.) All your research and everything anybody tells you will provide you with a better evaluation of it – and give you an increasingly logical perspective on the questions you may ask.

Before long it will be time to begin a rough plan of operation, but wait! The market – a newspaper – is the ruling hand in all your writing, and remains so in preparing for an interview. Your interviewee and the research you've uncovered will greatly influence the pattern you choose, for interviews come in several styles, like other writing. An old-fashioned formula is to compile questions more-or-less chronologically beginning with childhood and family life, and then continue with career-start and progress, problems, achievements and so on, according to what is relevant. This method still has its place as long as the pace doesn't drag (and it's difficult to prevent it doing so). However, for many papers there is neither space or reading-time to tell the interviewee's whole story. The average reader's attention span is limited, and if the first few words of the interview don't catch him he'll turn his eyes elsewhere. That 'holding' impact mentioned in the last chapter is just as important here. Only your market will tell you how much of the whole you can cover and of prime consideration will be whatever it is that makes your interviewee of interest to readers *at that time*. It may be a single aspect of his eventful life, or an important piece of knowledge he can provide on a topical issue. Your thoughts on how to plan which questions to ask must be tempered by this restriction.

Reminding myself it is not a good idea to ask anything controversial at the beginning, I generally get the plan into some sort of shape by writing down key questions as I think of them or as a particular item of research prompts me, on a large sheet of lined paper, leaving three or four lines between each question. This gives me room for more questions subsidiary to main ones, or lets me chop and change my first thoughts about as much as I like (and I always do). A good interview imparts information, preferably new information, about the interviewee to the readers; it is not just a question-and-answer session. 'What would I like to know about him?' is a good question to ask – and answer – yourself. The flow of questions should vary in length, complexity and perhaps most of all in weight, with avoidance of any questions requiring only a 'yes' or 'no' response. Thoughtful and caring questions indicate your genuine interest in your interviewee and his theme, and encourage him to expand on what he really thinks and feels, which is just what you want to hear. A relaxed atmosphere· will lead him to speak more freely and informally. Ideally, an interview should read like a spontaneous conversation. Questions that are predictable, dull or boring merely invite replies in the same vein. Worse, they bore your interviewee, often with disastrous results.

Of course you can't ask every question that occurs to you,

and selection raises its worrying head. If your interviewee is a well-known figure you may find a formidable amount of information about him – saddling you with a bundle of notes far too large to handle during the interview. What aspects of his life or work can you safely leave out? This is where a good memory, even a short-term one, is a blessing. Perhaps you (like me) daren't rely on it – so improvise with tiny *aides-mémoire* in your notes to jog you if the conversation takes a turn off the track you've planned for it. Looking up some of my old notes for interviewing an elderly painter I find 'Somme' and 'Boots' which were enough to remind me he had lost the hearing in one ear on the Somme and was one of the first men to be fitted with an artificial hearing aid, and that he was a distant member of the family firm of the ubiquitous high street chemists.

When I've shaped my questions as I think best I write them out again, and if I'm relying on shorthand or written notes I leave plenty of space after each question for the interviewee's reply. At an interview I also keep beside me a second sheet of paper reminding me about questions of lesser importance and this second sheet has an assurance value. I fancy I will remember the relevant basic facts about my man, and they may not be directly referred to in the course of the interview, but if they are and I've forgotten – see my second sheet.

The interview

Knowing you've arrived (promptly) with the tools of the trade gives you confidence; a notebook, your prepared and/or semi-prepared questions, a pen or pencil (and a couple of spares, remember Sod's law) and your portable tape recorder if you plan to use one. There are several good models available, incidentally, not all are expensive or difficult to work, and using one will free you from having to take your eyes from your interviewee and his surroundings.

A good battery-powered tape recorder is as sound an investment as a typewriter or word-processor if you're involved in a lot of interviewing. Reliability is paramount or the entire interview could be lost. You must be totally familiar with how it works and how long the tape lasts, for any mid-interview fiddling with a recorder (apart, perhaps, from reloading a fresh tape) is embarrassing to you and guaranteed to break the thread of what your interviewee might be thinking and saying.

You should be fully equipped, but do resist bringing all your armoury out at once and laying it on the table. That's enough to frighten all but the most robust interviewee! Ask if he is happy with the use of a tape recorder (unless you have established this point when you arranged for the interview to take place) and produce your tools casually over the first few moments while you're talking in a friendly manner before the interview begins. He won't agree to a tape recorder? Undoubtedly some people are inhibited by the realisation that a bit of electronic gadgetry is remorselessly docketing their every breath. If this happens you'll have to rely on your own writing; the weeks or months you spent learning shorthand will pay dividends, and with practice the speed of your best scribble will increase. I can't over-emphasise the value of learning shorthand: tape recorders have their uses, but they do not and cannot replace shorthand in every situation.

This is also a good time to check how long he expects the interview to last – and that you didn't forget your watch. Put that on the table as well if you will be able to see it less obtrusively there, or keep it on your wrist if you can look at it without him noticing.

If you will be taking notes by hand have the notebook comfortably on your lap rather than on a desk or table. You will be able to relax more easily and (more importantly) the distance your eyes have to travel between your notes and your interviewee's face will not involve constant dropping and lifting of your head. Even keeping him in the corner of your eye while you write on your notepad can be revealing; the less jerkiness there is between question and answer, the more natural the conversation will be – and the smoother the interview.

Make sure you can see a) him, and b) your notebook, especially if daylight has faded or will fade during the course of the interview. Resolve to speak clearly so he can hear you without any difficulty, and – above all – to concentrate. When you are both settled and there has probably been some initial small talk (but not too much) it will be up to you to set the interview rolling. Don't let much roll before establishing your theme, i.e. what you're there for, what it is that's going to interest your readers about this man, and what he's going to say about it.

If you've never met your interviewee before, it can be difficult to keep your mind on the job at the beginning. It is quite natural to be a little nervous; some interviewers like some actors, claim it keeps the adrenalin flowing for optimum performance. Once I interviewed a stage star whose handsome face I'd often seen in magazines, but a close encounter with this theatrical demi-god turned me weak at the knees. Could anybody be so devastating? He, long accustomed to interviews and swooning females, laughed and turned on more charm before I managed to clear my head and remember my assignment. It was one I thoroughly enjoyed, you can be sure!

On the other hand, if you find yourself reacting adversely to an interviewee who adopts a superior or semi-hostile attitude when facing the 'press' it's important not to show antipathy. You want to get something out of him, so a degree of 'rapport' is necessary, even if it can't always be entirely genuine. Strangely, after a job well done there might be a certain amount of grudging respect in the air; you may even have softened his earlier opinion about you and the paper you stand for.

Don't be so anxious about having your next question framed that you don't listen to what he's saying. Spot other points, too, that give you information without being put into words. As your attitude and tone of voice will affect the interview, particularly at the beginning, so will his. Experts in 'body language' will tell you crossing the knees towards another person is a sign of acceptance or interest in him. Gestures with glasses or cigarettes, and fiddling with hair or cufflinks or jewellery are very revealing if you know how to interpret them. (See Chapter 6 for details of an excellent book on the subject.)

Beware of subconsciously steering your questions in a direction that will ease the later writing of the interview if they do not naturally fall in such a pattern, and don't be frightened to acknowledge a mistake if you make one. If you find yourself inserting extra questions that didn't occur to you until you're face to face, fine. You're relaxing with a natural sincerity that will be welcomed and matched in spontaneous replies. He may also have been nervous when you started.

The side of a large lake in a remote part of Staffordshire was the setting for an interview I've never forgotten. My interviewee was a woman of mature years who had established a remarkable friendship with a family of foxes living near the lake, which was within half a mile of her old farmhouse. After our greeting I realised she was trembling violently. Why? We were on her home ground, at her request.

There was nobody else in sight, and probably nobody for miles around. It was broad daylight and there was nothing for her to fear. It came as quite a shock to realise the only thing she could be frightened of was *me*. Since then I've always made an effort to look at a forthcoming interview from the interviewee's eyes, and very often this has helped both of us.

In your stride, with the interview going well, you'll understand why I say interviewing is so enjoyable. You'll find yourself seizing unexpected openings, earning unforeseen bonuses with, perhaps, a confession of your own ignorance or an extra depth of understanding, and all the time you're at the centre of a fascinating and often heart-warming conversation.

One way to find yourself in deep water is to get side-tracked too far from your intended course. At all times you must be in charge of the interview and the direction it is taking, using a light and apparently innocent touch, guiding but never forcing your interviewee towards the anwers you hope he'll make. Push him and he may dry up on you. Be aggressive and he'll prickle. Being in charge does not mean being inflexible, and sticking rigidly to your plan could make you miss those informal gems he'll let slip when he's at ease. It will help to let him lead at the emotional level for it is at these times – often late in the interview when you can ask a 'risky' question almost as if you've only just thought of it – that he might give you some of your most valuable information.

Often a moving recollection or response is best greeted with nothing more than a nod or gentle smile, for there is a time to keep silent in most interviews. He could need a short break (and so could you) to recover himself, and as long as it doesn't last too long this can be useful; while he organises a cup of tea, lights a cigarette or just blows his nose, you will be catching up on what's gone so far and what's coming next.

Enjoyable as interviewing is (well *nearly* always) you are there to do a job and nothing better can drop into your lap than a revelation. Your interviewee springs some big news: he got married yesterday, he's running for Parliament, he's left his wife of thirty years – or whatever, in his context, is news. Suddenly you have a news story as well! It can't be wasted in an interview that might not be printed before next week – and you have all the research material about your man.

Writing it up

You go home with a bundle of notes, a couple of full tapes and a headful of images; you can hear his voice, visualise his mannerisms, feel the friendliness (or otherwise) of his house and taste the almond on his wife's fruit cake. How is all this to be translated into a written interview? This is the third part of interviewing.

Back to reality and you recall your job is for a newspaper, which means catching the readers' attention immediately. Consulting your original draft for the interview may give you some of your structure, but after the interview you will be ready with a fresher, closer and brighter start. Indeed you may decide to abandon all your first thoughts and intentions. The enthusiasm and spontaneity that rubs off a charismatic interviewee is invaluable in carrying you through the writing-up of the interview, as long as you don't get carried away. You were there and your readers were not, so your task is to make them feel they had been; that it was they, not you, who heard your interviewee's voice, felt his friendliness and even tasted his wife's fruit cake. And if 'he' was a gorgeous blonde, they want to 'see' that as well.

Did your interviewee say anthing to make a good opening quote? 'I love getting married. It's being married I don't like' was my intro to an interview with a thrice-divorced stage personality currently dating a youngster half her age. This had been her answer to a question she had mused about without any prompting from me. 'I suppose you wonder who my next will be?' Her eyes undressed my paper's forty-five year old photographer and flickered away. His face was a picture. Another good opening might be something that made you laugh during the interview, recorded either directly or indirectly, or an aspect of the interviewee that particularly moved you and will move readers. However you begin, plunge right in!

Despite the limitations of a narrative style it has a few advantages worth borrowing in moderation. You can set the scene of where the interview took place to help readers picture it, you may skip over less interesting periods of your interviewee's life or experience and you can intersperse direct quotes with information about his background, where appropriate. You can also use flashbacks as long as they do not take over the main stream of the write-up.

How much of 'you' is there going to be, and how are you going to present yourself? Are you to appear as a friend, a colleague or just a disembodied and even unidentified voice? And how are the questions to be posed – every one in direct quotes ('What do you most want in life?') or occasionally dropping into indirect speech ('I asked him what he most wanted in life?') to avoid monotony?

On the whole nothing makes an interview alive on the published page better than direct quotes and (bearing the balance of the copy in mind, as above) the more you can include the better; for these you'll bless your tape recorder. Writing all or part of the interview in the present tense may also keep it light with a friendly impact. Beware, nonetheless, of being too informal, lest readers feel you have treated your interviewee flippantly, especially if the theme, i.e. why you are interviewing him, is of a gentle or serious nature.

Your deadline may determine how soon you write up your interview but I advise doing it as soon as possible while it's still fresh in your head. This gets the job done and out of the way, leaving you free for other work, and lessens the danger of involuntarily imagining something was said when it wasn't. Did he mention such-and-such which you didn't write down, or has the thought supplanted the words because you hoped to hear them? There's nothing like words on paper for reassurance if you didn't use a tape recorder.

Surprises

Perhaps it is the unpredictability of interviewing that gives it that special satisfaction but I can't pretend the surprises you might encounter are unfailingly welcome. Unwanted distractions can wreak havoc with your carefully planned half-hour. Your interviewee may fancy a couple of floppy spaniels on the sofa, a background of fortissimo Wagner and boisterously inexhaustible toddlers given free access to the interview. How tolerant should you be? A wife/mother/secretary may break in with messages, requests and general diversions. Do you smile gamely through them all for fear of upsetting your interviewee? That is another reason for fixing your interview location as tactfully as you can in the first place! A friendly greeting or pat on the head to interruptors on two or four legs is one thing: an interviewee constantly distracted and not properly listening to your questions, or giving merely surface responses, may be an interview ruined.

Another alarming custom favoured by those well-practised in the business is the 'multi-interview'. You have assumed it will be a one-to-one affair, but no; you arrive to discover a 'minder' or two is to sit in the room with you, perhaps even answering up for your interviewee or fending off questions he doesn't like. Usually in these circumstances you won't be the only interviewer either, so it resembles a mini press conference more than an interview. This could be a problem. If you do find this happening to you, without any forewarning or contrary to what you may have been led to believe would occur, I'd advise you to cut your losses and leave. You won't be missing much for any exclusivity will be lost. A press release will supply whatever your editor might want to see about your potential interviewee, if he's still interested; a write-up from a press release is a very different animal from a live interview.

Where a child is involved as an interviewee, or in an important supporting role, it is expected that a parent or adult will be present. In these circumstances you will have to trust that a) the adult does not interfere or restrict the course of your questioning, and b) your own reserves of gentleness with the child and patience with the adult will be adequate!

A top newspaper interviewer I spoke to when preparing this chapter told me that only once, during more than forty years of interviewing, had he been threatened about what he must or must not write. He demurred, the threat was repeated more sternly and my colleague walked out. No interview was published. As for bribes, 'No such luck!' laughed my friend. Both, of course, are to be treated with the one response the interviewee doesn't want – exit.

A request that you should keep a particular statement 'off the record' falls into a different category. I dislike being put in this position, for I am being asked to lay aside the interviewer's hat and – for a few moments, perhaps – be a personal friend. It's not that I don't want to be friendly (I usually do) but the interviewee is suddenly and unjustly assuming control of the interview. For decency's sake I am obliged to observe whatever confidentiality is to be kept, and I do so, albeit feeling that the interviewee has taken advantage of me and my position.

Vetting your draft

You've finished. The write-up is complete and you're ready to file it to the paper. Just a minute! Did you say anything to your interviewee about letting him see what you'd written before it goes for publication? Frankly, I hope you did *not*. It's a tricky point and I well understand the comfort of knowing he's satisfied with your copy. That way, you might assure yourself, there will be no complaints, denials or misinterpretation about what he did or did not say or mean. Bits he wants deleted can be cut out, in other places you can amend your copy to accommodate his second – or third – thoughts and anything he would like rephrased is easily altered. Above all, you'll be in·the clear.

NO, please! The accepted ethic in journalism is not to let your interviewee vet your copy except in purely factual matters, if necessary. It may be, for instance, that he doesn't have an exact statistic at his fingertips while you're talking to him and would like you to include it. Then, of course, it would be unreasonable to refuse him the chance of making a later addition.

This practice of not letting an interviewee revise your copy is not due to stubborn pride or any sense of superiority about what you've written – Heavens, any journalist fancying his copy is sancrosanct would last no more than a day in this business. But newspapers are about people. Imagine the delays if all copy had to be checked (possibly in long-winded detail) by the people it concerned; I doubt tomorrow's paper would be printed before the middle of next week.

There's another reason: to let your copy be 'passed' by someone else – someone who is hardly the best judge of what he may have said about himself – will be undermining your own credibility. If we don't learn to take interviews (and do any other newspaper jobs) and then practise and polish our skills, we will be wishy-washy writers indeed, of no particular value to any newspaper. That doesn't mean our early interviewees must be sacrificed for our own career-interest, but the reverse. Knowing (or assuming) the interviewer is *capable and confident* of doing a good job, will give greater confidence to an interviewee as well.

All the same, complaints occasionally arise after an interview is published. 'I've been misquoted!' 'We never mentioned it!' 'The interviewer made that up!' There is little to be done when this happens. No editor wants to be involved in disputes and it could boil down to taking your interviewee's word or yours. You have your notes or tapes to support you if necessary, but the editor is the arbiter and should be your ultimate support. He knows you, your reliability and your standard of work. Yes, he knows you can also make mistakes; you are human, as is your interviewee. Unless matters reach a crisis (which seldom happens) nothing official will be done other than sending a polite reply to the interviewee regretting the receipt of his complaint; you may never even know there was one.

'Distant' interviews

Is it necessary to meet someone face to face for success? Interviewing by phone and even by correspondence is often done but in my opinion nothing beats going and seeing for yourself. The best interviews get *inside* interviewees, which leaves telephone interviews out in the cold. A 'conversation' by correspondence may be a little closer to the real thing. Yet in both these circumstances the word 'interview' takes on a different meaning; one may be the only way you can get a direct quote, the other could be a legitimate avenue of research for a personal profile, and both are perfectly valid means of communication. But unless you are extremely talented and/or experienced, both will lack the impact and immediacy that gives your published copy sparkle and makes your readers feel they, too, were talking to the famous.

There's one small task to do after the interview is published, and it doesn't take more than a moment of your time. Write a brief 'thank you' note to your interviewee and slip in a copy of the published interview in case he hasn't seen it. Then you're ready to move on to your next one.

6
Help and Where to Find It

When you're still struggling with your first article or beginning to fear you'll never get anything published you may think an established freelance has a secret recipe hidden from you. Only when you get to know him better do you have an inkling of what goes on behind the scenes. Maybe he doesn't tell you how many books he's consulted to find a single piece of information, that an obscure statistic took three months to track down, where he chanced on a notably bright anecdote, or how he managed to interview a celebrity who had hitherto refused to speak to the press. You don't hear about his cuttings files painstakingly garnered over the years or his precious 'contacts' book of people who can tell him what he wants to know or at least point him in the right direction to finding out. Oh yes, he's got a recipe and if it's secret that is only because it's individual to him.

Part of the help you gather round you as your writing life progresses will also be personal and of use only to you. Your own book of contacts, for instance, is worth a great deal. It will carry names of people you've found who can and will provide you with valuable information, listed with where to find them and just what help they provide. I am no artist but I know where to turn for essential artwork or pix in a hurry – or I can be confident that if my contact can't help me quickly, she'll know someone else who can. Often one contact will lead you to another in this way, and so your contacts increase and the book becomes even more valuable. Parting journalists from their contacts books is like depriving babies of mothers' milk.

Your cuttings file

Second only to a contacts book in a do-it-yourself system comes your private cuttings file. This will also grow with time and very soon it will become your best friend, because nobody will have exactly the same file to refer to. I'm not saying you'll be at a disadvantage quoting facts other journalists quote (facts are facts after all) but if you can support your quotes from your own cuttings file your copy will stand out as at least original and at best unique. Building your own file is not difficult; many writers are compulsive collectors of snippets of information long before they've thought about what use they're likely to be. Every newspaper you read, every book or magazine that comes before you, everything anyone says that just might come in handy, you either snip it out, copy it in your notebook or jot it down on the back of your hand. Easy, isn't it? Yes, until....

Cram everything you find into an old envelope and you could be filling it with trouble as well. The first precept of taking a helpful cutting is to give it a *date* and a *source*. Only then should you file it – *in its right place*. If you're collecting willy-nilly you may prefer to ignore the last instruction and fill the envelope with everything, promising yourself you'll have a grand sort out at a later date. Fair enough, if you wish. But I still advise preparing a departmentalised cuttings file and putting your cherished cutting in the right place at the start. Why make yourself unnecessary work? It doesn't matter how primitive your file is; a load of old envelopes clearly labelled but held together with a rubber band or in a shoe box will serve the purpose. Better and easier to manage as it grows fuller is a concertina-type file with large identifiable pockets that are easily renamed. As your cuttings file enlarges you'll realise you need to make subdivisions of some sections, so off you branch into more envelopes, shoe boxes or concertinas or box files. However you do it, keeping to an ordered system is one thing you'll have cause to bless frequently in the future.

Quoting your source on the cutting itself, i.e. where you found it, is important and can make the difference between a helpful and a doubtful one. As for putting a date to it – that is, to my mind, *vital*. Supposing you dug out a cutting giving population figures in Manitoba, say, before 'last year's census'. The cutting has no date on it, so when was the census? How accurate are the quoted figures now? You don't know and you daren't (if you are wise) risk using it. There's only one thing to do with a cutting like this: tear it up. You might be tempted to use it and could land yourself in trouble because you relied on the unreliable. Furthermore, it has wasted your time and space, so a cutting without a date is worse than no cutting at all.

A final word about your own cuttings file: let it be a servant but not a master. It's possible a cutting is incorrect, isn't it? Whoever wrote it might have made a mistake and by relying on it without question you could be perpetuating that mistake. So check it, unless it's quite impossible to do so. And if that happens, well, whether you use it or not might just depend on what you had for breakfast or whether it's raining; it depends how you feel. If you decide not to risk it, something else in the file will set you off on another trail if you want one. (Frankly, I can't imagine any writer could be short of inspiration when looking through cuttings, for my problem is having far too many with not enough time to use them.) A cuttings file will ensure you never run out of ideas.

Research

Supposing you are writing a 'help' article and want to use an incident where a tourist had his wallet stolen in Bombay. Could you advise other travellers what to do in such circumstances? How can you find out about foreign currency limitations, tourist regulations, and where to go for assistance when you have been robbed in another country? These and many other questions will need answers – accurate, up-to-date answers – before you can think about how to write your piece. All you need to know (in this and at the start of almost every project) lies in a single word – research. In the first instance, that usually means consulting reference books.

Editors report that inadequate research is the prime reason for rejection – and sometimes checking what you *thought* you knew is the first task, as I discovered from browsing in a dictionary. Like other readers I assumed ecu to be a newly invented word; not so apparently. To us it is an acronym for European Currency Unit but to French ears it is an old gold or silver coin and used to be a common name for the 5-franc piece.

Market guides

Research begins with finding the market and there are several handbooks listing titles, addresses, phone numbers and other details about newspapers. Some are published annually, and therefore cannot keep pace with day-to-day or even month-to-month changes, but (that restriction part) they are thorough and reliable:

Writers' & Artists Year Book.   **A & C Black**
Recommended by the Society of Authors, this long-established vade-mecum is in two main sections: markets, and general information for writers.

The Writer's Handbook.   **Macmillan/PEN**
Rapidly establishing itself as a reference for all those concerned with the creative world of writing, the latest edition has many additional entries, including the latest schedules of rates for freelance journalists.

Willings Press Guide.   **Reed Information Services**
Available for consultation in Public Libraries, as is the one below.

***Benn's Media Directory* (formerly Benn's Press Directory), Benn Business Information Services Limited, PO Box 20, Sovereign Way, Tonbridge, Kent TN9 1RQ**
Here are all the newspapers in the UK, both national and regional, with circulation details, key management, editorial and advertisement executives. Cover prices and advertising rates are also listed.

***British Rate & Data,* Maclean Hunter House, Chalk Lane, Cockfosters, Hertfordshire EN4 0BU**
Media facts are at your fingertips in this (expensive) monthly publication which is primarily a marketing handbook. Its comprehensive coverage includes all national and regional dailies, Sunday papers, free regional dailies (there's only one so far), weekly papers, freesheets – and even ships' newspapers.

A–Z of Free Newspapers & Magazines, **Ladybellegate House, Long Smith Street, Gloucester LG1 2LT**
This may be obtained by post, but is also expensive.

Freelance Market News, **Freelance Press Services, Cumberland House, Lissadel Street, Salford M6 6GG**
A monthly publication mainly covering magazines.

UK Press Gazette, **Quadrant House, Sutton, Surrey SM2 5AS**

Journalist's Week, **City Cloisters, 188–196 Old Street, London EC1V 9BP**
Two weekly publications for journalists.

Books

Getting the facts correct is the essence of credibility in all writing. The first step in this is providing basic statements of fact on which to build research. Consulting a reputable encyclopaedia is a good starting point. The first mentioned below adds the pleasure of colour and clear non-technical language to more than 1,000 pages of world events, history, arts and sciences:

The Hutchinson Concise Encyclopaedia **Century Hutchinson Ltd.   £15.95**
With tables and charts, illustrations and maps, many in full colour, this superb volume is an indispensable guide to the modern world. Among its 17,500 entries you will find new nations, financial terms, sporting greats, the human body, wildlife habitats, sports and how they are played, the latest scientific and technical terms – and much more.

Pears Cyclopaedia   **Pelham Books Ltd.   £12.99**
Smaller but of great practical value, this densely-packed book is arranged in some 20 sections, from 'Prominent People' to 'Medical Matters', 'Classical Mythology' to 'The Environment' – and more. An invaluable asset to anyone's reference library.

It is important to keep your method of research up-to-date. For guidance on how to set about it you won't find a better or more comprehensive book than:

Research for Writers **by Ann Hoffman published by A & C Black.   £6.95**
An invaluable handbook that is now an established tool of reference, offering a wealth of first-class guidance and information. It is no exaggeration to describe this book as essential to every serious writer. Through its pages you will be led to research in every field – and merely reading *how* to pursue your particular trail will whet your appetite to begin.

For clarity of writing

There can be nothing more important than a top-class dictionary. Several recently-published volumes are available and if you haven't looked at a modern one you may be in for some pleasant surprises. These are my favourites:

Concise Oxford Dictionary **£10.95** *SET*

Published in July 1990, the eighth edition is much larger than its predecessor, has more than 20,000 new entries and is as up-to-date in content and presentation as it is possible to be. It has been completely redesigned for greater ease of use, and the definitions have been rewritten in straightforward everyday English, with an absolute minimum of symbols and special conventions. Ideal for the 1990s, it includes entries needed for copy about the lives we lead, such as 'cardphone', 'community charge', 'kissogram', 'global warming', 'viewdata' and 'user- friendly' (yes, it is, too). Among the particularly useful appendices is a succinct guide to punctuation and its usage.

19-95

Chambers English Dictionary **£17.95** ✓

This is a dictionary for the space age, yet retains the comforting reassurance of a well-loved friend. It's a treasure chest for word lovers ('sharny', 'poodle-faker', 'coolamon') and you'll find yourself looking them up for the sheer delight of doing so. Besides new words are literary words from the Bible, Shakespeare, Dickens and major 20th-century writers. There are business and financial terms ('golden parachute', 'Chinese wall', 'white knight' and 'poison pill', for example), scientific and technical terms like 'E numbers', 'thunderhead' and 'AIDS', and all entries have easily understood definitions and uncomplicated pronunciation guidance. There's more: if you don't know the size of A4 paper, for instance, the size used in the UK for virtually all copy, you'll find the answer in one of the handy factual appendices.

Besides these fine volumes, the following give the word 'dictionary' new significance:

Collins Concise Dictionary Plus **£8.95** *SET*

This is not just a dictionary, it is Collins Concise Dictionary *Plus* more than 15,000 encyclopaedic entries set alphabetically *in the text*. As if this weren't enough, almost a couple of dozen supplements cover the animal kingdom, the British monarchy, consumer durables, political Britain 1945–87, causes of death in Britain in the same period, countries and their leaders – and much more. An excellent reference tool obviating the need to consult a separate encyclopaedia at every turn.

Collins Dictionary and Thesaurus in one volume   **£13.95**
With a similar dual purpose to the above, this is a dictionary and thesaurus in dictionary form, conveniently arranged so that the relevant material from each entry appears on the same page. This means that definitions, spelling, pronunciation, usage and a wide range of *substitutable* words are instantly available without the need to consult a second volume or indeed to search in other parts of the same volume. From 'abaft' to 'zymurgy', invaluable.

Inevitably a thesaurus not linked to a dictionary will be more comprehensive, and this one has special attributes:

Chambers Thesaurus   **£6.95**
Drawn from the *Chambers English Dictionary* database, this paperback word-finder is the perfect memory-jogger; it helps the writer struggling to encapsulate his meaning in a forgotten *mot juste*, and is most valuable to journalists, writers and reporters. A good thesaurus like this has a special fascination; every use enhances your personal command of words and increases your general knowledge. But its greatest attraction lies in giving a list of possible words that have more of a particular ingredient – or less, are more formal – or less, are more euphonious – or less; that, in short, have more – or less – of the precise flavour sought by the writer.

Other reference books

There are so many useful reference books I could fill one just listing others. It is always worth consulting those published years ago as well as more recent arrivals on the scene. This being so, you may not easily find what you want (but read on). Here are just some of those I particularly recommend, old and new:

A Concise Dictionary of Confusables
Hodder & Stoughton   £4.95
Was the villain 'hanged' on the gallows, or 'hung'? Is 'proficiency' the same as 'efficiency'? Does 'supine' mean 'prone'? To settle these and any other confusions, this is the book to buy.

The Concise Oxford Dictionary of Quotations   **£4.95**
The Concise Oxford Dictionary of Proverbs   **£3.95**
The Concise Oxford Dictionary of English Etymology   **£14.95**

The above three should be on every writer's desk.

If you can't always say what you mean these may solve your problems:

Mastering Practical Writing by S. H. Burton   £3.95

Mastering English Language by S. H. Burton   £4.25

Mastering English Grammar by S. H. Burton   £4.99

Three most useful little books in the Macmillan Master Series, providing a brush-up on what you may have forgotten.

Chambers English Grammar by A. J. Taylor   £2.95

A handy little reference book providing a simple introduction to the 'nuts and bolts' of English grammar.

Teach Yourself Correct English by B. A. Pythian   Hodder & Stoughton   £4.95

An excellent buy if you're hazy about how formal or informal newspaper writing should be. 'The ordinary user of English would do well,' advises the author, 'to copy the better features of journalistic writing: crisp, clear English, directness of statement, and sentences of digestible length.'

Chambers Idioms   £4.95

Another little gem. The use of idioms and figurative expressions in our richly expressive language will lift your copy, by enlivening your style of writing. But this book is more than a list of idioms; knowing the origins of many adds to a writer's understanding and ability to use them. With this dictionary English will be all plain sailing.

Chambers Dates   £5.95

Yes, a book of what-to-write-about – but with a difference. This book covers such a diversity of topics (politics, literature, sport, business, people, exploration – you name it and it's almost certainly here) that it's a fine prop for all seekers after general knowledge as well as a ready reference. With more than 6,000 important dates listed, there should be enough variety for us all.

A Journalist's Guide to the Use of English   Bottomley/ Loftus   £2.00

Newsman's English by Harold Evans   Heinemann   £9.95

McNae's Essential Law for Journalists by Tom Welsh and Walter Greenwood   Butterworth   £10.50

These three are not geared to beginners but will be useful at any stage.

Teeline Shorthand Made Simple by Harry Butler   £3.95
Learn shorthand to ease and extend your working life!

Body Language by Allan Pease   Sheldon Press   £4.95
Invaluable information for interviewers, and a useful guide at any time to what people are feeling – which may not be the same as what they are saying. Interpret other people's thoughts by their gestures, learn how to tell if someone is lying, and much more. Written by an international expert on 'communication without words'.

Finally in this section, I can't speak highly enough of a paperback to treasure and refer to constantly:

The Oxford Writers' Dictionary   £5.95
Described as the 'essential style guide', this paperback is for all those concerned with writing style and the printed word. Do you write 'council-house' or 'council house', 'Romania' or 'Rumania', is it 'gypsy' or 'gipsy' – and should 'vice versa' be in italics? While your market will be your first style guide, this handbook not only provides the answers (in default of others) to such questions as these, but also deals with familiar and less familiar abbreviations, broader aspects of usage such as capitalisation and punctuation, foreign words and phrases, proper names of people and places – and how *not* to spell commonly misspelled words. How did I ever manage without it?

Where to find the books

An invaluable source of help, although not a publisher himself, is a well-known Fleet Street bookseller who is the leading stockist of books on journalism and related topics, with writing a strong speciality. It is well worth sending for his catalogue:

L. Simmonds, Bookseller, 16 Fleet Street, London EC4Y 1AX. (071 353 3907)

The National Council for the Training of Journalists at Epping (see next chapter) also has a large holding of useful books and tapes. Ask them for details.

What do you do if you know a book exists but you can't find it? Luckily for researchers there are folk who specialise in solving this very difficulty. You could try one of these:

Geoff Fitzgerald, Jubilee Books, 203B Locking Road, Weston-super-Mare, Avon BS23 3HG. Tel: 0934 633166
This 24-hour *free* service is one of the best in the UK, the only cost to the enquirer being postage on any books supplied (plus the price of the books, of course). Supply the title and author of the book you're looking for, and if possible the date of publication and publisher, although this is not essential. Jubilee can find books on any subject. Novels, rare books and magazines come within their scope and their sources are constantly updated. They also have contacts in most countries throughout the world. Because the service is a full-time business results are as fast as may reasonably be expected.

Bookfinders, Camberley, Moor Lane, Westfield, East Sussex TN35 4QU. Tel: 0424 754291
Another free service, depending for their income on the sales of books they find.

Bookwatch, Peter Harland, Bookwatch Ltd, 15-Up, East Street, Lewin's Yard, Chesham, Bucks HP5 1HQ. Tel: 0494 792269
A specialist in anything to do with books. Publishes bestseller lists and a weekly publication titled 'Books in the Media'.

Research services

The Dewey Decimal system is widely used in Public Libraries to catalogue books in ten main subject classes, and understanding how it works will save writers time wasted by looking in the wrong place. Any librarian will be pleased to explain it to you (it is easy to learn) when the place is not busy. Most borrowers and readers who use the reference departments make use of only a small part of what is available to them; more delving into what's on offer could be a welcome eye-opener. Many writers have little idea of what is available until they 'discover' the joys of their Public Library. Just set aside a few hours to getting to know the way round yours, and it could be the most valuable time you've spent in all your research.

The library you find most useful may well be the one in your own town, but there are plenty of others available.

All major newspapers house their own libraries of press cuttings taken from their pages as it is the task of several employees to snip every separate topic and file it away. Writers have cause to rejoice that they do so for enquirers to newspaper libraries are (in my experience) generally treated efficiently and courteously. Few demand that the enquirer be a member of the staff although a commissioned or contributing freelance may be given more consideration than a stranger. If the library staff do not know you, be sure to tell them you are commissioned to write an article for the paper or have been invited to submit one, if that is the case. Mentioning the editor or features editor has suggested you contact the library will remove any doubts. Anyone with time-wasting, amateur or unreasonable requests may not be well received. Enquiries should be succinct, clearly stating the date or approximate date of the required cutting or cuttings and when you need the information.

Unfortunately what may be a free or inexpensive service to those with good contacts is likely to cost unknown beginners hard cash. 'Shall I risk it, then?' you may ask yourself when faced with the choice of paying for reliable information or making an educated guess. I'd have to reply: No. Your reputation now *and in the future* might be the price you have to pay after all, and it could take years of hard work to recoup that.

News International Library   Tel: 071 782 4000
For papers in this group a commissioning letter is required before you may make free enquiries.

Daily Mirror Library. Chief Librarian Alan Hemple   Tel: 071 353 0246
Phone at least three clear days in advance to make a personal appointment as telephone requests and unscheduled callers are not welcomed. Part of a day or a full day in the library costs £40.

Financial Times Library. Librarian Paul McCluskey   Tel: 071 873 4652
A fast and efficient service covering most topics and personalities. You pay for faxing material, generally at a rate of £50 per time (credit cards only) depending on the service required.

British Library Newspaper Library, Colindale Avenue, London NW9 5HE   Tel: 071 636 1544, extension 7353 for general enquiries
Housed almost opposite Colindale Underground station (with some offshoots in other parts of London) this is the largest library of its kind in the world. Access is by ticket only, which must be obtained in advance. Researchers are normally expected to go to the library in person or to send someone on their behalf. Helpful assistants take a deal of trouble over genuine requests. Newspapers prior to 1801 and weeklies are housed here.

Press Association Library, 85 Fleet Street, London EC4P 4BE   Tel: 071 353 7440
More than *fourteen million* news cuttings are now available from the PA, the National News Agency of the UK and Republic of Ireland. Here you may find cuttings on every conceivable subject covered from every imaginable angle. There is also a collection of daily events listed for the past five years, 'who said what' quotes for the last year, and an outstanding selection of standard reference books. For personal visits call the News Librarian on 071 353 7400 to make an appointment (£20 per hour or part thereof); for commissioned research, call the same number and give a detailed brief (£28 per hour or part thereof). Helpful librarians give their (free) advice on what is available and how best to research your subject.

BBC World Service Shop, Strand, London   Tel: 071 257 2946
For top features journalists are offered 'newspacks' of research material produced to high editorial standards. These are handy 'quick fix' binders on a country or topic with over *10,000* facts in each pack and regular updates with all the latest information.

Hans & Edda Tasiemka   Tel: 081 455 2485
A large cuttings library started as a private enterprise when this couple were working as freelances. Updated daily and run on fully commercial lines. Prices from £20.

Tracking Line, 23 Spearhill, Lichfield WS14 9UD   Tel: 0543 254748
Organiser Rod Richards runs a research and information service specialising in police and criminal history, biography and source location.

Organisations and associations

An association exists for absolutely *every* trade, interest and occupation – if only you can find it. And if you can't, the DBA can. It is the *Directory of British Associations* and its coverage of associations alone, for instance, runs to 3845 different headings, subdivided into all you ever wanted to know about your subject plus a great deal more you never dreamed existed. 'No human interest or activity,' it claims, 'is too specialised or exotic to lack a society or group, and the subject index to DBA is the key to them all.' Although I could argue with the wording of that statement I can't deny the DBA's omniscience. Its abbreviations index alone is daunting, and a lesson to all writers not to assume readers know what abbreviations stand for. What do a bricklayer, a dentist and someone with a hearing difficulty have in common? The answer is BDA – but not the same BDA. Those initials stand for at least eleven different associations, and in this case they are the Brick Development Association, the British Dental Association and the British Deaf Association. Turn DBA's pages and the indices point you to a huge quantity of compressed information, so much that you'll find it hard to stop researching once you begin. There's just one snag: the newest edition (10), called the *Directory of British Associations & Associations in Ireland*, costs £90. But libraries will stock it if the demand is strong enough for them to do so. There are similarly colossal editions covering sources of statistics, management, councils, committees and boards, European professional and learned societies, centres and bureaux, European industrial and trade associations.... For more details contact:

CBD Research Ltd, 15 Wickham Road, Beckenham, Kent BR3 2JS.

Wot, no charge?

Some of the most helpful advice available to everyone is overlooked simply because it is free. You have a query about a particular word, its usage and origin? Here's the solution:

The Oxford English Dictionary **Word & Language Service, OUP, Walton Street, Oxford OX2 6DP   Tel: 0865 511544**
A team of researchers will find what you want to know through the database of the *Oxford English Dictionary*. Marvellous!

Other help can come from an army of public relations folk who are out there just waiting for your queries. PR officers or departments of industries, tourist boards, arts associations, volunteer support groups, political parties, environmental organisations – it sometimes seems the world is only too anxious to give you useful information, and it's all free. Contact the promotions or PR department of associations and organisations relevant to your subject and you may find yourself inundated with material.

CATFAX   Tel: 071 436 6392   9 am to 6 pm any weekday
Perhaps cats are one of your special interests, as they are mine. This is a free information service for any media enquiry about our feline lovelies. They even offer a photographic library as well. (My cats are not included, I'm sorry to say.)

In our environmentally-conscious time the phrase 'free as air' may no longer be appropriate, but *World Climate Change Report* will cost you nothing. Contact:

BNA International, 17 Dartmouth Street, London SW1H 9BB

I think so-called junk mail was invented for my delight. Everything non-writers might toss in the waste paper basket with nary a glance I pore over eagerly. Free *useful* information lands on my doormat daily by the see-through wrapperful, and long may it continue to do so. Do you read yours? In the past few weeks I've had brochures about holiday insurance and seasickness cures (handy for an article about travelling to the Scillies), facts and figures about tooth decay (could help an item about mouth health) and information on the Mongolian wild horse (well, you never know…). I've never directly sought the junk mail that comes my way. I don't have to. But if anybody ever says 'Tick here if you'd like to be on our mailing list', I tick.

On-line with your computer

Even if you're not using a computer or word-processor for your writing it's important to know what can be done with these modern marvels. Perhaps that is why more and more freelance writers are making technology work for them.

As in the rest of life, it's a matter of each to his taste. A few weeks ago a bright young sales rep from one of the leading software houses tried to sell me a program that would paint my prose (*all* my prose, it appeared) with a coat of what he called 'class'. Programs to check for spelling mistakes are commonplace, although only the most sophisticated (and expensive) can pick up 'there' where it should be 'their' (let alone 'they're') and most writers with an instinctive feel for spelling find them at their most useful winkling out two words running together and therefore reading as one. But 'Buy this program,' he assured me, 'and you will be writing like Shakespeare'. For newspapers? Thinking of posterity, let alone the sanity of editors and publishers, I didn't buy the program.

Word-processors have replaced typewriters in many homes and an inexpensive computer could give you the power to 'key in' to your local library, scan its catalogue, check facts, find quotations and much more – without ever leaving your house. I say 'could' because some extra equipment is necessary, but the basic system is neither costly nor difficult to use. With a modem, which resembles a small box, you can go 'on-line' to search libraries – anywhere – that are equipped for you to 'viewdata'. This method of library researching saves days and even weeks of working time and puts information at your fingertips, or, more precisely, on the screen in front of you. With your ability to save information on disk you can of course also keep it to refer to again.

Enquire at your library to discover whether your local authority offers an on-line service; if so it may work 24 hours a day, for it is all done by computers which know no set hours. Should you be in doubt about how to use such a scheme, how it works or how much it will cost, ask a senior officer of the library service to give you details. Most major libraries will at least supply information about viewdata services.

Get on-line and you can have on your screen far more than access to libraries. The next step is getting information from the many companies that give it out – for a fee – to anyone who wants it. No further hardware is needed; a personal computer, a modem, the required communications software and a telephone line do the job very well, although being able to search through these on-line databases can be expensive; the companies charge an annual or monthly fee for allowing you access to their data 'banks' – and, of course, you have telephone charges to pay. But move up-market like this, and you may gain access to information never available through press cuttings or libraries, however specialised they may be. Once you've sampled what is available, you'll realise the benefits are mind-boggling. Don't be deterred by the word 'database'. It is nothing but high-tech jargon for a huge filing cabinet into which somebody has put facts and figures which can be revealed to you via your home computer. Dozens of companies now exist whose task it is to fill the databases for you. *Reuters Textline* offers business and financial information based on over 1,000 publications all over the world. *Meridian* is a Parliamentary information system. Many of these high-powered databases offer access to others. *Dialog*, for example, will get you into hundreds of scientific and technical databases and *Lexis* is the legal storehouse. Log into *BBC Data Enquiry* and you can get virtually *any* information you need – at a cost of £60 per hour plus VAT, minimum fee £34.50 for half-an-hour's research. You want information that may be contained in any of the publications deposited in the British Library since 1950? Search for it the 'old' way and you might need to be another Methuselah; get on-line to *Blaise* and what you want can be on the screen in front of you in minutes. Such apparent miracles are hard to believe until you've seen them in action.

At the time of writing the price of computer hardware and software is falling and the services on offer to writers are increasing in number and usefulness. The whole of *Roget's Thesaurus* is now accessible to home owners of Amiga, Amstrad PC1512, Atari ST and IBM PC compatible computers. The program is based on the Longmans Pocket edition, contains over 150,000 entries and is available on 5¼" or 3½" disks. There is also an easy-to-use indexing program for Atari ST authors. Details of these and other programs are obtainable from:

Kuma Software, 12 Horseshoe Park, Pangbourne, Berks RG8 7JW. Tel: 0734 844335

To home-based writers this high-tech wizardry means press the appropriate keys on a computer and all the information you want appears on the screen. Thousands of millions of press cuttings (I exaggerate not) will electronically disgorge themselves at your command (one at a time, in dozens, or as you want them), on-line services await your bidding and archives can be nuzzled for as long as you wish. Didn't I say 'mind-boggling'?

Office and secretarial help

If you're desperate for help with typing, word-processing, photocopying and other purely practical aids, *The Production Centre* in London is the place to go.

The Production Centre, Threeways House, Clipstone Street, London W1

Here you will find help of every type, but perhaps all you want is a desk in peace and quiet that you may book by the hour. However modest your needs you have all the facilities of the Centre at your disposal during your stay. As well as this the Centre can provide a mailing address and telephone answering service, help with the preparation of scripts, prepare a budget for your accountant and offer advice about almost any problem concerning writing.

The London Writing Rooms, Farringdon House, 105 Farringdon Road, Clerkenwell, London EC1R 3BT

For less than £40 a week you can rent a private work room in London with your own key, the use of a kitchen and an outgoing telephone.

Richmond Business Centre, Tel: Pat Schooling   081 948 5771

Also offering working space for 2–3 people on a daily or weekly basis.

Finsbury Business Centre, Robert Gibbins   Tel: 071 278 0333

Barley Mow Workspace Services, Chiswick, Netta Livingstone   Tel: 081 994 6477

These two accommodate longer-term tenants.

The Workstation, Tony Orsi   Tel: 071 490 2382

For writers under 25 who want working space in central London with phone and access to communal fax and photocopying facilities for just £20 a week.

Personal help

For advice and help in your writing there are several criticism services at your disposal. It must be said they are of more value in long-term training than for immediate help:

The London School of Journalism, 19 Hertford Street, Park Lane, London W1X 8BB   Tel: 071 499 8250
Criticism is given on many types of writing and advice offered for a prearranged fee.

Writing is a lonely business. Meeting others of like-mind may be more than an opportunity to get away from the word-processor or typewriter; it may broaden outlook and strengthen resolve. Only you can decide what you want. You may find members of writers' organisations and societies a spur or a bore; helpful or hopeless; not to be missed or to be avoided like rejection slips. I can only tell you I know several well-established writers who have never forgotten the help they received from such groups in their early days. Here are details of some societies and associations:

National Union of Journalists, Acorn House, 314 Gray's Inn Road, London WC1X 8DP   Tel: 071 287 7916
The largest union in the world for professional journalists, numbering more than 33,000 members of which some 6,000 are self-employed. Part of the NUJ Code of conduct requires members to 'avoid the expression of comment and conjecture as established fact, and falsification by distortion, selection or misrepresentation', meaning that they should not pretend that matters of opinion are matters of fact.

There is a London branch solely for freelances, while others are attached to branches in other areas of the country. Prospective members have to be proposed and seconded for membership by existing ones. If you don't know any contact Head Office for information about your nearest branch meeting where you will surely find some. Freelances in all ways receive the same treatment as staff employees on newspapers and magazines, and are eligible to receive unemployment pay from the union regardless of any other kind of benefit they may be entitled to claim. Subscriptions are geared to income and you will never be expected to pay more than you can afford. The union publishes a freelance directory. Minimum rates of pay may also be negotiated with employers.

Institute of Journalists, Chris Underwood (joint General Secretary), 2 Dock Offices, Surrey Quays, Lower Road, London SE16 2XL   Tel: 071 252 1187
This organisation has fewer than 3,000 members with the

freelance section the largest and most influential. A press card is issued to members, as is assistance with legal and other problems.

The Society of Authors, 84 Drayton Gardens, London SW10 9SB   Tel: 071 373 6642

Open to journalists as well as authors. Fee £50 for the first year, then less. A quarterly magazine titled *The Author* is sent free to full members and for a fee of £10 per year to non-members.

The Society of Women Writers and Journalists, Mary Rensten (Membership Secretary), 13 Warwick Avenue, Cuffley, Herts EN6 4RU

A 95 year old society of professional and amateur women writers in every field.

The Press Club, 76 Shoe Lane, London EC4A 3JB   Tel: 071 353 6207

Membership is open to all journalists whether freelance or staff employees. There is an initial entrance fee; thereafter subscriptions, on a sliding scale, range from about £30 to £70 per year.

Writers' circles are the starting point for many freelances. Among their members you will find writers of all sorts but one thing you can count on: whatever type of writing they do they will all know the regional or local paper – and that is often where budding newspaper writers begin. I've found every group I've ever visited immensely friendly, but only you can judge whether the one you attend is going to be of value to you – or whether it is just a talking shop of mutual and meaningless self-congratulation.

If you would like to join a writers' circle but don't know of one in your district, you may find what you want in a directory that lists over 600. It cost £3 post free and is available from me thus:

Directory of Writers' Circles, Oldacre, Horderns Park Road, Chapel-en-le-Frith, Derbyshire SK12 6SY

Most writers' circles number amateurs among their members (who can start as anything else?) but some groups want to remain amateurs and pursue their writing purely as a hobby.

Here is a well-known example:

British Amateur Press Association, Mr L E Linford, 78 Tennyson Road, Stratford, London E15 4DR
A long-established gathering of proven worth.

But perhaps you are miles from anywhere, have no means of transport or are quite unable to leave your home. What about a correspondence course? For newspaper work this is particularly tricky because by their nature papers are quick, in both senses. It is for this reason that this book urges you to get out in the marketplace and sop up all the newspapers you can absorb until the ink gets in your blood. Try doing that by post and even the best teacher's advice may be dry when you get it – making the copy you write cold and behind the times (*sic*).

The best tutors by mail are accredited to the *Council for the Accreditation of Correspondence Colleges* which sets out to maintain high standards and is undoubtedly of practical and proven help, notwithstanding this disadvantage. Naturally they are not without critics. One much-advertised school in London, for instance, was the subject of an attack in *The Observer* in June 1989 when a picture of Malcolm Bradbury was captioned: 'These schools are preying on the aspirations and dreams of individuals who are never going to make it.' The paper also cites the case of a lady who won £100 in the same school's magazine story competition but had to turn to the Society of Authors for help. She wasn't a member at the time, but only obtained the money due to her after a fight by the Society. Its General Secretary believes the spate of complaints it is asked to handle must be merely 'the tip of the iceberg'. The Council for Accreditation of Correspondence Colleges stated 'if they (the school criticised) hadn't left (the Council) themselves, they would have been asked to go and they knew it'. This was followed by complaints from other such bodies that the criticism had loosely included writing schools in general. Potential students can only listen to the opinions of fellow writers – and try for themselves.

There are many residential and non-residential schools and conferences in this country, where writers of all types gather to socialise and learn more of their craft. So numerous are they that I have space to mention only one – the largest, probably the oldest and certainly the best-known. This is the Writers' Summer School held in rural Derbyshire for six days every August. Further details may be acquired from the Secretary. She is:

Philippa Boland, Writers' Summer School, The Red House, Mardens Hill, Crowborough, Sussex TN8 1XN   Tel: 0892 653943

Regional arts associations regularly host lectures and tours by established writers – watch your local or regional press for details – and courses for writers are often organised by WEAs and local councils. The service organisation for all thirteen regional arts associations in England (Scotland and Wales have separate Arts Councils) is:

Council of Regional Arts Associations, Litton Lodge, 13A Clifton Road, Winchester, Hants SO22 5BP

The National Institute of Adult Continuing Education, 19B De Mountfort Street, Leicester LE1 7GE   Tel: 0533 551451
Write to Jane Morris of the Publications Department for a copy of *Time To Learn*, (price £2.50) which includes details of courses for writers.

General interest

Here are some addresses any freelance might need sooner or later:
The Press Council, 1 Salisbury Square, London EC4Y 8AE Tel: 071 353 1248
This was replaced by The Press Complaints Commission in January 1991, as the first stage of the 1990 Calcutt proposals.

Campaign for Press & Broadcasting Freedom, 9 Poland Street, London WIV 3DG
This is a pressure group working for more accountable and accessible media in Britain.

The Newspaper Society, Bloomsbury House, Bloomsbury Square, 74–77 Great Russell Street, London WC1B 3DA Tel: 071 583 3311

Department of Trade & Industry's Small Firms Service Telephone 100 and ask for FREEFONE ENTERPRISE.

Central Office of Information, Hercules Road, London SE1 7DU   Tel: 071 928 5037

Arts Council of Great Britain, 14 Great Peter Street, London
SW1P 3NQ   Tel: 071 333 0100

Public Record Office, Ruskin Avenue, Kew, Richmond,
Surrey TW9 4DU   Tel: 081 876 3444

Keeping secrets

This chapter can't hope to mention all the thousands of
avenues of research that are available. When you've done all
you can for your piece and made use of every scrap of help
you can find, and your copy is written, does the research
show through? Is it apparent to readers that you've been
raiding libraries, filling in facts from reference books and
quoting from cuttings that have already been seen by too
many eyes? Always remember that research used well can't
be seen. And the best researcher keeps his secrets.

7
But How...?

'How do editors like to be approached?' 'What if they don't pay up?' 'Where do I syndicate my work and is it worth it?' 'Could I get proper training in journalism?'

This chapter answers these and other questions.

'How should I submit copy to newspapers?'

Although nobody would pretend the appearance of an on-spec manuscript can make the difference between acceptance and rejection, there is no doubt clean and clearly presented copy is more satisfactory for everybody who handles it. Even commissioned work is better received if it looks easy to read; a sub-editor will approach neat copy more happily and be less likely to chop it about in sheer irritation. It hardly needs saying that your print should be crisp and clear – so discard worn out ribbons on typewriter or printer.

Neatness means double spacing on one side of A4 paper, allowing wide margins all round (3 cm, say, and perhaps 4 or 4½ at the top of the first page) with pages numbered, preferably in the top right corner. The first page is generally not numbered. Type 'more' or 'mf' at the foot of pages other than the last and finish your copy with the word 'end' and the wordage.

There is no rule about how the number of words should be displayed and common sense will be your guide. It is usual to quote to the nearest ten if under 100 and in 50s from 100 upwards. So 87 would be 90, 164 would be 150 and 1,263 would be 1,250. Never add 'approx', as if you might be sued for miscounting. It is also wise to type your name, address and phone number on the last page below your copy and the wordage.

Start the first par at the left margin but indent subsequent ones 3 spaces and do not leave an extra line space between pars. There should be only one character space between the end of one sentence and the beginning of the next. If you use a word processor do not justify the lines at the right margin.

Give your copy a heading and if it is a long piece (approaching several hundred words or more) break it up on the page by inserting 'crossheads' in the text at suitable intervals. This is particularly important if your work is unsolicited, for editors thrive on headlines and a rapid skim through crossheads gives them an instant notion of what your copy is all about. Neither the headline nor crossheads may be used as you set them but they will help the copy look more appealing on the pages. There is no way you may know how they will be used on the printed page (for you do not know where your copy will appear, nor what may flank it on either side) but at the submission stage what you are aiming for is ease and speed of reading.

You'll also need a 'catchline', which is a word or phrase at the top of each page beside the page number. Its purpose is to identify where your page belongs should it be separated from its fellows, and the catchline may be anything you wish. Choose 'cream', for example, for each page in an article about catering, and your pages will be numbered 'cream 3', 'cream 4' and so on. Any catchline will suffice, but be original at Christmas when there could be confusion if other writers also choose 'Christmas'!

If you're used to submitting to magazines you may be surprised to learn that on the whole newspapers do not like finding a 'frontispiece', a 'title page' (call it what you will) attached to the front of the copy with details of who you are, what you are writing about and so on. They are more interested in getting to the point – and that (they hope) is to be found in the first par on page one. So I recommend putting whatever you have to say about an 'on spec' article in a brief letter and then plunging straight into your copy. Like this:

Dear Mr Bloggs,

As a lecturer in Hotel Management at Sally Lunn College I enclose a 1,000 word article on the local job opportunities for young people in the catering industry, with details of practical training courses here and in the rest of Europe. An SAE is also enclosed.

Yours sincerely . . .

Of course that important but brief letter will begin by reminding an editor that he commissioned the enclosed copy (if that is the case) on a stated date.

That's all, except that any previous success you have had with the paper should be referred to if it was long enough ago for the editor to have forgotten. Unless your telephone number is pre-printed on your headed notepaper do not make a point of providing it, for an implied hint that the editor will rush to phone you may be misconstrued. Particular mention of rights offered will brand you as a true amateur and may also be thought of as arrogance on your part (see Chapter 8).

Copy begins on the next sheet. Cut off any spare paper on the letter sheet so the fact that your copy starts without any more preamble is immediately apparent.

For your own peace of mind you will want to keep a copy of your work, known as a 'black'. Carbon paper is messy but effective and NCR ('no carbon required' paper coated with a special substance that obviates the need for carbon paper) is popular but expensive. I use an excellent paper called 'Action' which is cheaper than NCR and works just as well. There's nothing like a duplicate in your hand for the comfort of seeing what you've submitted but I confess I rely on storage on a computer disk for short pieces, or for items I know will be published within a day or two. *This may be considered dangerous and I do not advise it unless you're prepared to risk losing your copy altogether!*

Use a pseudonym? If you wish to do so, no paper will object – but make sure the accounts department knows about it so you have no problems with payment.

The frequency of publication will determine when to send your copy. Your subject may also affect it, and you will need to allow extra time for the placing of Christmas and other seasonal work. An editor may be more kindly disposed towards you and the world in general on a Monday than on a jaded Friday, and a quick phone call to his secretary or the telephone switchboard (if there is one) will tell you when he's coming back from his holidays. Maybe your copy will be enthusiastically received if it's the first he sees on his desk that morning.

Finally, the packing and postage. For two or three A4 sheets it is enough to fold them over once and use a 23 × 16 cm envelope. For more A4 sheets a larger envelope that will take them without folding is preferable. Do not forget to enclose a self-addressed envelope of the same size, adequately stamped. Long study of our postal system convinces me the Post Office is so haphazard about deliveries of mail that life is too short for second class stamps. I always send copy first class, even when it is in no great hurry. I know it costs a few pence more each time, but if you're in business, you're in business....

To allay worries that your copy didn't arrive you could enclose with it a stamped and addressed postcard for someone to return to you, although few newspaper offices will be bothered to do so. It is better to phone the editor's secretary a few days after posting to check that it did arrive. If she knows about it, *resist the temptation to ask any further questions!* Should you hesitate about asking whether they have your copy or not (lest the editor consider you a nuisance before he's even read your work) you could send your copy by registered or Recorded Delivery if you wish to spend money – or by P326 if you don't. P326 is the number of a *free* service provided at main Post Offices. It does not cover registered or recorded delivery letters. All you do is complete a pink form which the counter clerk will date stamp and initial and return to you. If you ever need any proof that you did post your copy on a particular day, just wave your P326.

'I've been told to ring in with my copy but how is it done?'

Copy is usually taken over the phone when there is not enough time for it to be filed in the normal way, for instance in the morning after an evening event when a report is wanted for a daily or evening paper. Ask beforehand if you're not sure what time to file (i.e. ring the paper with your copy) or which number to call. When the time comes you will need to be prepared with either your complete piece ready to read out over the phone, or with notes you feel adequate. On this latter point let me warn you, from long phone-filing experience; reading a 'finished' piece from notes is not easy and there is absolutely no time on the phone for 'Oh, no, change that to...' or 'Er, that's wrong. I'll start the sentence again...'. So (until you've had long practice and only then if you're confident notes will suffice) get what you want to say written down before you touch the telephone. You needn't type your copy or write it out neatly, for nobody but you will ever see what you've written. A scribble (but a *legible* one) on any paper is all you need. I've spent years covering live stage shows and use the time driving home, usually late at night, to plan my overall piece. Getting the first sentence straight in my head sets me off to a good start when I get to a piece of paper, even if the rest is vague at that stage. Sometimes I file the copy about midnight (if I know the copytakers on duty during the night!) but usually it goes at about 8 a.m. the next day.

Whether your copy is a news story, a report on a meeting, a review or whatever it is, have it in front of you and dial the number you've been given to reach the copytaker. When she answers (I've yet to find a male copytaker; perhaps they're not up to it) remember the single most important rule: *make sure she has your name* with your phone number if the paper doesn't already know it. This may seem mercenary but many a good story taken over the phone finishes with a quick "Thanks, 'bye" from the copytaker and nobody but the reporter knows (or wants to know) whose story it is. That vital point established, say 'I've got a report on a Council meeting', or 'Here is a theatre crit' or whatever will give her a quick idea of what's coming – and begin.

Read your piece clearly and in phrases, giving enough of each phrase for someone who has no idea what you're going to say next to understand it. I've always found copytakers uncannily acute and quick. Usually she will say 'Yes' or grunt or just wait (you'll probably hear her keyboard-clicking pause) for your next phrase. If you get off on the wrong foot and each is waiting for the other to go on, just ask her to indicate when she's ready for you to continue. You'll soon get into the right rhythm. Be careful to spell proper names, words offering ambiguity (unless their usage makes their spelling obvious) and anything else not plain from your text. There is no need to labour over punctuation (that's what sub-editors are for) except to refer to 'point' or 'full point' (house styles vary, even on the phone) at the end of sentences, 'new par' when you're starting a new paragraph, and to say 'quote' before direct speech and 'close quote' after it. Tell her when you've finished and say goodbye. Don't ask for a read- back or if there are any queries, for she probably has half a dozen other people queueing up to file their copy as well, especially if it's first thing in the morning and everything has to be put to bed by half-past nine.

Only when you read your copy in the paper a few hours later may you realise that a mistake could easily have been avoided if you had thought to spell out a word here or use a different phrase there. Writing copy to be filed by phone is itself special; do it often enough and you'll find yourself instinctively avoiding words that might be misunderstood – and that can only be good for us and our writing skills.

'How should I write to an editor with my ideas?'

On the whole, 'query' letters fall into two groups: those sent before submitting copy, and others chasing it (commissioned or not) after it's been posted. Let's deal with the first category. It is sometimes possible to write for a newspaper in the same comparatively leisurely time scale as you might use when writing for a magazine, i.e. when a known future event lets you write what is referred to as 'magazine' copy. The 1990 World Cup in Italy, for instance, is being contested as I write this; it has given freelances plenty of scope for associated copy in virtually all newspapers, where articles are being published on every conceivable aspect of football.

But for most newspaper work the pace is crisper; more topical (if not 'today') copy is required. There is simply not time to write to an editor asking whether he would like to see your piece. When speed is important it is better to query by telephone. Whichever way you decide to make contact, take enough time to prepare your proposal. After all, this initial query could earn you a large fee, so don't rush in ill-prepared. Be ready with what you want to say, in the same format as when writing the piece itself; state what it's going to be about without cautious preamble, then give the editor or his representative (the features editor, maybe) details of its proposed length and viewpoint, if one is appropriate, and outline why you think it will suit him just now. Don't get carried away and offer more than you can be sure of delivering. But don't be hesitant about your professional ability either; if you have little confidence in yourself, why should he (who may not even know you) have any at all?

Now for the 'chasing' letter. Imagine you've submitted copy to a paper 'cold', or 'on spec' or without any previous contact about it, and you didn't take any steps to find out whether it was received. Weeks and months go past and you've heard nothing. Should you query the paper about it now? Of course if the intended recipient reports not having received it any proof of postage you obtained at the time will be no help and its non-arrival will only concern you and the Post Office.

If you decide to query it, it is better to do so by letter rather than by phone. Write to the editor's secretary (on a national or large regional paper) or to the editor himself clearly stating the circumstances and enclosing a stamped self-addressed envelope for a reply.

More time goes past and nothing happens? Then phone the same office and explain your difficulty, mentioning your earlier letter. If, despite all this, the paper is uncertain about whether your copy was or was not received, you could assume they don't really want work from freelances. Luckily there are plenty of others who do – if you're in time. All that remains is to list the one that didn't respond to the chase in your private Black Book.

'Shall I call on the editor of my local paper?'

Without any prior contact – NO! Editors are busy folk and sometimes those on the smallest papers are the busiest, having to do many jobs themselves.

If he has said he'd like to see you, ring the paper and ask when would be a suitable day and time – and don't be late. Never suggest meeting anywhere other than in his office! Whether the meeting is his idea or yours, take it as an indication that he is interested in your work and sees (or hopes to see) you as a useful contributor to his pages in future.

Be prepared with tear-sheets of your work, especially newspaper work. It is wisest to let them speak for you, although he may not give them more than a cursory glance, but of course you could refer to whatever previous newspaper experience you may have had if it is relevant to do so. Give some thought to what you want to offer him as occasional or regular contributions and (if appropriate) produce some written ideas. Leave them with him if he's interested, rather than expect him to study them on the spot.

Talking to an editor face to face can bring practical benefits, so don't be shy. In discussing what you're going to write for him he's bound to reveal his own likes and dislikes and his personal view of the topic in question. When he actually sees it in print a few days later, he will recall the conversation and (assuming you've followed his lead) is likely to look more favourably on your copy.

If you don't know the current rates of pay, ask. No editor will think any the worse of you for doing so, in fact most will instantly raise you to the 'professional' category at such a question. When the reply is, 'Our usual rates,' it is easy to tell the truth. 'I could be out of date, so please tell me what they are.' Embarrassment when talking about money is as much an invitation to be paid less than your due as is demanding it before you've demonstrated your ability to file good copy. In the first case you could be taken for a ride, in the second suspected of thinking the fee more important than the work, which is a mistaken priority.

Don't get so interested in what an editor's saying that you forget the time. He can probably only spare you a few minutes – and if you keep him from his own work for too long he might recall you as a potential time-waster rather than a valuable contributor.

'What is a commission and how do I get one?'

'Get a commission,' a bright-eyed novice once told me, 'and your troubles are over.'

Well, I seldom write 'on spec' and my troubles are still there. But they are different troubles.

When you get talking to an editor and he discusses your forthcoming copy, listen carefully to what he says. Is his interest in your idea the same thing as a commission? And what, precisely, is a commission (or ordered copy, as some papers call it)?

It is a written or *verbal* agreement that you should go ahead and write whatever it is you've suggested or the paper has suggested to you. It is *not* a half-suggestion, an idea tossed about in the course of conversation or a concept more-or-less understood from what someone wrote or said (and perhaps *mis*understood by that person later). If you have suggested (by letter or phone) that you write an article for an editor on a particular topic but are not sure from subsequent correspondence or phone calls whether you have a commission or not, establish your position before you write your copy. Simply ask, 'Have I a commission to write...?' Commissions are often ordered over the telephone and are just as valid as if they are on a piece of paper in your hand. If you obtain written confirmation, so much the better.

The importance of being certain when you have a commission is not for mere satisfaction with the job immediately ahead, agreeable though that may be. It is a legal two-edged contract that makes the obtaining of the next one easier – providing you fulfil your part of the bargain – and helps strengthen the professional relationship between you and your commissioning editor. He relies on you and you do a good job for him.

Journalists have no agents when they work on newspapers and have to speak up for themselves. I don't work with an assumption that editors are going to do-me-down and I hope others will not take such a cynical view, but there are times, alas…and the thorny question of was-it-a-commission-or-not is one that sticks into most of us sooner or later.

To have someone argue that it was only a commission if the editor (or someone with his authority) contacted you and asked for the work is nonsense, just as is the case if payment is withheld because the commissioned piece was never used. Let me emphasize that it is only the minority of newspaper editors who may cause you trouble. The majority are fair, hard-working, as honest as most of us, and are frankly too busy to create problems out of sheer cussedness. Because 'getting a commission' is a matter of working practice that can (and does) cause resentment between writers and editors, it is very important to get the matter straight from the start – with an agreement about your fee and what expenses you may also claim.

'How do I make a career out of newspaper writing?'

More than half of all journalists now working learned the craft 'on the job', i.e. they have had no formal training. Recognised schools and colleges cannot take all the young hopefuls keen to enrol as trainee journalists, but in some respects it is no handicap if you can't get any official tuition. Determination is one of the more desirable qualities in journalism, and this will be your greatest asset, whatever your age.

There are two ways a school-leaver may begin, and one is as a trainee with a local newspaper. Getting such a job is not easy, and making a direct approach to a local editor could be the best road to success. Market guides like Benn's *Media Directory* (see Chapter 6) and reference libraries may also help you find an opening.

The other route is to take a one-year pre-entry course at one or other of the dozen or more colleges offering this facility. Further information about such courses may be obtained from:

National Council for the Training of Journalists, Carlton House, Hemnall, Epping, Essex CM16 4NL Tel: 0378 (Epping) 72395

Completing a course cannot guarantee you a job on a paper or even that you will regularly turn out acceptable copy (although you should be able to by then) but you will have taken several important steps up the ladder. Some local education authorities or newspaper groups sponsor students in their college year, meeting all or part of the cost of the pre-entry course, and a few groups run their own training schemes. The recently proposed National Vocational Qualification (NVQ) aims to raise the level of proficiency among trainees and lay down standards required to turn them into competent regional journalists. Defined points of attainment are envisaged: making routine enquiries and originating ideas, planning and carrying out assignments, writing, presenting and filing copy and accuracy in shorthand to a standard of 100 words per minute. There is (at the time of writing) much debate about who should assess what is required and how the new scheme will compare with the existing criteria practised by the NCTJ.

Not everyone approves of the NCTJ courses. East Midlands Allied Press (known by its acronym EMAP) is one newspaper group that prefers to train its own recruits, and there are others that also ignore the NCTJ.

Postgraduate entry into journalism (and about half the people entering local newspaper work have a degree or some equivalent qualification) provides further options: you may take a postgraduate course in journalism studies at the University of Wales, College of Cardiff, for example, or at City University, London. There is also a post-graduate 20-week pre-entry course (recognised by the National Council for the Training of Journalists) run at the South Glamorgan Institute of Higher Education. Apply to any of the above for details.

Those aged between 24 and 30 who find direct entry onto a paper the only route will not be indentured as trainees but will be registered with the NCTJ. If you start above the age of 30 you will not be registered at all, so it is important to see that your training is adequate – and here the NUJ may provide invaluable assistance.

If you are starting in your middle years or later and want occasional or regular work as an 'out of the office' freelance, don't consider any lack of training a disadvantage. The NUJ is now seeking to run courses for freelances, both newcomers and established journalists, and will supply further information on request. Freelances who were staff journalists first might claim the skills they learned and the contacts they established give them a head start, but fortunately the passing years endow us all, if only we let them, with an unbeatable native sense, a firm spirit of application to the task and all the opportunity we could possibly wish for. Self-employed writers work in news agencies, public relations, on magazines and in broadcasting as well as on newspapers. When you really want to do it, nothing will stop you.

Regardless of your age, there are several working aids you will find worth their weight in copy; if you haven't yet acquired them and nobody is likely to teach them to you, I strongly advise you to do-it-yourself. The most valuable is shorthand. There are several systems and I still use one I learned many moons ago. It is based on word sounds rather than 'squiggles'. Whichever sort you choose you will always bless the day – let me not be too euphoric, the few weeks or months – it might take you to learn it.

Can you type at speed using all nine digits? (Yes, in traditional typing the left thumb is curiously redundant.) If you can't, teach yourself from any reputable manual. It's not difficult and when you've mastered it you'll get through five times as much work as you did with the old two-finger 'Where's the apostrophe got to?' method. (An extra refinement that I learned so long ago I can't remember where, is a keyboard shorthand that lets me type as quickly as I can think!)

'How do I know whether my accepted work was ever published?'

Assuming you don't see the paper regularly you could: (a) ask friends who do to look out for your copy, (b) persuade someone working for the paper to do the same, (c) ask the editor's secretary to send you the relevant copy(ies), (d) contact the cuttings library, if there is one, or (e) ask the editor to tell you exactly when your copy will be published.

Course (a) is probably the best if you have reliable friends who see every issue of the paper. You might opt for (e) which sounds trouble-free, but in my experience not all editors want to bother with copy once it's gone. Both (b) and (c) could be wild shots if you don't know anyone on the paper, which leaves the most hopeful course (d), the cuttings library.

Regional provincial and national papers will provide you with a photocopy of your work on request, but what if the paper doesn't run to a cuttings library? You may resort to one of the cuttings services mentioned in Chapter 6, for which you will have to pay, of course.

If everything else fails, luck may solve the problem. Once, when I'd missed an edition of a paper carrying some copy I particularly wanted to keep, I opened a well-packed parcel sent through the post – and there among its protective wrapping was my copy. I can't recall what was in the parcel but I certainly welcomed its packing!

'Should I send an invoice, and when may I expect to be paid?'

Always send an invoice for newspaper work, for if you don't it's most unlikely anyone will ever pay you. An invoice is a simple bill, made out on your headed paper for preference, stating the title you gave the copy (if it has not yet been published) or the heading they gave it (if it has), the date and the sum owed to you. Here's another reason for getting all details sorted out before you write a word; if a fee hasn't been mentioned you may not know how much to invoice for. An entirely speculative submission may have been accepted and you genuinely don't know the fee, so you could make a guess and hope whatever figure you quote will be paid. This sometimes works but tends to fix rates for future sales to the same paper – and you may begin to wonder if you should have asked for more the first time!

As for when to send your invoice: the sooner the better. To many freelances that means even including it with the copy. I prefer to invoice a paper a few days after filing commissioned work and immediately after publication if work has not been commissioned. The former I pursue to the death, if necessary, as all commissioned work earns (or should earn) a 'kill' fee if it's not used. Published material that was not specifically ordered must also be paid for, of course.

The practice of newspapers not putting your invoice through the accounts system until a month after the piece has appeared is regrettably commonplace. All too often this means your item appears in print in, say, the first week of July but you don't get paid until the end of August, i.e. the beginning of September. Even then perhaps you'll still be waiting because – guess what? – half the accounts department is on holiday. Be grateful it isn't Christmas, when things are often worse! Some papers even process invoices quarterly, meaning four months might elapse between seeing your work in print and getting paid for it. If you are on a commission for a series or a regular column, make sure there is a firm agreement about when you will be paid before you begin work. And the one-off story that you still haven't been paid for? Keep pushing, politely but firmly. You may be told the paper is waiting for some artwork or other material to accompany your copy, or that a new story broke unexpectedly and for the time being yours has been held over.

'How can I obtain payment due to me?'

Send a letter to the accounts department explaining how much you are owed and for what, giving the date and all relevant details. If nothing happens after what you consider to be a fair time (three weeks is more than tolerant) write a cool and lucid note stating the amount you expect to be paid, and that you plan to take the matter to the local County Court if you have not received full payment within ten days of the date of your letter. Send this last letter by Recorded Delivery. Writing 'Recorded Delivery' on the letter itself emphasizes its importance to whoever reads it when the covering envelope bearing the 'Recorded Delivery' sticker may have been thrown away.

Your letter may convince the publication you mean business. If it doesn't they will be chalking up another small mark against themselves when the case comes to court – if it ever does. For although you must be prepared to carry your threat through once you've made it (if you don't you will be allowing the baddies to win again) many potential baddies miraculously turn into goodies at the prospect of legal action – and pay up like lambs.

The true nasties, and fortunately there are few, may get their own back or kid themselves they've won by paying you less than they owe. Unless large sums are involved it is generally best to ignore such petty practices; if you're not content to do this a solicitor will advise you as to whether you should still take the case to court. Then it will be important to name the right person or persons against whom you are claiming and to sue only for the exact sum you are owed, plus any expenses included in your agreement. Proof of the assignment or contract is, of course, immensely valuable. Editors may not realise that when they offer you a commission they are putting the job in the frame of your working practice, i.e. your house rules, and if the matter of non-payment ever comes to court, the dispute will be viewed in that light, to your advantage. One Manchester freelance has taken twelve publications to court in the last few years without any cost to herself or any union for legal fees; I don't think papers knowing her track record in the courts will be dilatory about paying her full due in future.

'What are all these lovely "freebies" I hear about?'

Get an assignment to report a flower show or the Royal opening of a hospital wing and someone will have to provide you with a ticket for the event or you may not even be admitted. On an official job (where the organisers want the publicity a newspaper report will bring) it would, of course, be foolish to expect you to buy your own ticket, stand in a queue at the gate, and so on. You receive your free admission ticket and off you go. Usually there will be another ticket for a friend (any photographer from the paper will make his own arrangements) and this may be considered your first 'freebie' – a little extra treat for a friend who has to do nothing. You do the job, file your report to the paper, and that's that. Or is it?

It may be more complicated – delightful, you may think – when organisers shower you with other freebies during the course of the job and generally treat you so well you feel somewhat obliged to write only nice things about them and their event. How could you mention most of the flowers had withered and visitors complained there was no tea, or that the hospital wing was dirty and the Royal patron was seen by nobody but a handful of officials, disappointing the crowds who had waited for more than two hours in a muddy field? Wouldn't it be ungrateful to write nasty things when you and your friend have been given bouquets of flowers, plants for your own gardens, the offer of a greenhouse at cut price and all the cream cakes you could eat?

There is only one answer. Don't get in such a predicament in the first place. Entrance tickets are freebies to accept without comment, of course, or you might not be there to do the job, and the extra ticket for a friend is also quite acceptable. So is a cup of tea, say, if the occasion is suitable, and even a sandwich or a bun shouldn't compromise your conscience. These are normal social pleasantries, after all. Beyond that, beware! A sensible perk is one thing, a privilege for being in the position of doing it is (probably) all right, but before accepting anything ask yourself if the giver sees it as a bribe, albeit such a word would not cross his lips. And when the answer may be 'Yes' – decline.

At theatre reviews you may be given the best seats because the publicity manager wants you to see and hear the show properly: fine. As a book reviewer you will be given the books to keep when you've done the job: again, that's normal practice (the only paper I ever found that expected its reviewers to hand them back '*in pristine condition!*' soon found itself short of reviewers). But once I was offered a blatant 'reward' to write a glowing account of a newly published book. I was gratified to learn some months later that the publisher had gone out of business. (It wasn't even a well-written book.)

Freebies are an acceptable part of the job in certain circumstances. If anyone piles them on to excess I become embarrassed, squirm to get away and am reluctant to write a word. So 'all those lovely freebies' can be self-defeating. Like all journalists I expect what I write to be paid for; in pounds, thank you, not freebies.

'I'm petrified of libel. What is it?'

Although we value the 'freedom' of the British press, newspapers have no legal right to publish absolutely *anything* they like. In everything journalists write the laws of libel and contempt sit as watchful shadows on their left shoulders. (Left? Most are right-handed and that is too busy reaching for reference books, cuttings, the phone, etc., to let anything balance on their right shoulders.)

Libel concerns anything which might be defamatory, i.e. injurious in the eyes of the paper's readers to the reputation or good name of someone now living. As the size of libel damages awarded in the courts grows, papers are getting increasingly nervous at incurring them. The tabloids are generally the offenders. In December 1988 *The Sun* paid out £1m to Elton John (making the reputed £100,000 they paid to pop singer George Michael in May 1989 almost a relief) and more and more papers are fearful of getting put out of business by settlements of this size – or even larger. Plainly in the light of such events all papers are being a great deal more careful about what they print, even if they can turn proceedings against themselves to their apparent advantage by making bigger publicity out of the story in the next issue.

That may be putting a brave face on things, but libel hurts, and nobody can pretend it doesn't. In America it is almost a national sport; dozens of papers add disclaimers to their horoscopes, reminding readers horoscopes are *entertainment* and are not based on any proven scientific facts.

Editors try to sleep calmly at night by calling on lawyers to read any article they are doubtful about before it goes to print, and up to now the big nationals have been able to afford legal advisors or have their own staff lawyers whose sole task is to check everything for libel. Even then, as these and other enormous compensation payments show, mistakes are made. Some of the big papers can afford the huge premiums of libel insurance but they, like all other publications, are worried.

It has reached such a pitch, and so much money can be at stake, that cynics allege some managers and agents for the stars in the entertainment world deliberately scour the tabloids looking for potential libel actions. The majority of cases are eventually settled out of court for 'undisclosed sums' and at one end of the scale there may be big money in it. But far more people are not so well-known; for them, bringing a libel case against a newspaper ends in nothing but heartache. How many 'little' people feel themselves libelled but are too frightened to take court action must remain a guess.

Libel is extremely difficult to define, and even harder to prove. Defendants may be able to plead justification, or that the item was fair comment. What you consider damaging to your reputation may not be thought harmful by other people, and the very law of libel is wholly based on individual cases as they come before the courts. So when you hear of a newspaper being sued over offending passages you can be sure the litigants have taken sound legal advice and know what they are doing. Bringing a libel suit against a newspaper (or anyone else) can be very expensive indeed, and for libel no legal aid is available to anyone.

Incidentally, as a matter of precision, it is not the publication of an offending passage that is in dispute. Libel may exist only when the passage has been published, is found to be defamatory *and has been circulated to a third party*.

Individual journalists who are members of the NUJ or IoJ can obtain insurance cover against libel quite inexpensively, as each of these organisations will explain on request. The fear of libel should not keep writers awake, though a working knowledge of what it's all about is valuable. On the whole the larger the paper you write for the less you need worry, and

nearly all smaller papers are part of larger groups. Common
sense is the best guide and if you write anything that you are
anxious about a word to the editor will alert him. Of course, if
you take this to mean you may write the most scurrilous
articles about all and sundry and expect the editor to put you
right, he will – by rejecting your work and refusing to consider
it in future.

'What is meant by Contempt of Court?'

Newspapers are barred from publishing anything currently
the subject of court action on the grounds that material
printed might prejudice the fair hearing of the case in
question. The 1981 Contempt of Court Act has wider
implications, not all of them as readily understandable as the
above. It can be used as a purely legal mechanism to block the
press for months or even years on a matter of obvious public
concern. *The Sunday Times* was prevented from publishing its
investigations into the effect of thalidomide, for instance,
despite a long, exhausting and costly effort to print the truth
as they saw it for countless anxious readers all over the
country. A case of the law of contempt being used to hide a
cover-up? It was an added irony that by respecting the law we
couldn't discover the truth. Newspapers are always sceptical
about the use of law, particularly the law of contempt, when it
works against them. 'Just a telephone call,' complains *The
Sunday Times* editor Andrew Neil, 'makes it easy for a judge to
get a gagging injunction, and they have become now the
single biggest threat to the freedom of the press in this
country.

You may not plan to be a full or even part-time staff
journalist working on a newspaper but a brief knowledge of
the law, as it concerns the press, will be of more than passing
interest to writers of all varieties – and can be of practical help
when you least expect it. The Official Secrets Act of 1989 limits
the range of what is regarded as 'secret', while the code of D
(Defence) Notices is a voluntary practice with no legal
backing. D Notices are merely formal requests seeking to
curb, in the national interest, what newspapers are about to or
would like to publish. Voluntary they may be, but if a paper
ignores a D Notice and publishes whatever was thought to be
'secret' the editor may be liable to prosecution. Further
information about these and allied topics is to be found in
McNae's Essential Law for Journalists (see Chapter 6).

'What is syndication?'

Every freelance quickly learns how to make several sales out of one. This is quite legitimate and merely involves 'rejigging', i.e. rewriting the original copy, perhaps adding fresh material to bring it up to date, or writing it from a different angle, and – hey presto! – there's an altogether new item to send to market. You are, in effect, plagiarising your own work, and as you own the copyright of it, you are quite entitled to do so. Elsewhere in this book I mention how I have made full use of most of the material I originated in newspaper columns over the years. Some of this copy has since been syndicated in regular slots or corners in regional and small-circulation weeklies around the country with very little extra effort on my part.

Wouldn't it be easier to sell the *same* piece of work several times, without having to alter it to disguise it from its parent? This is not only possible but ethically acceptable, and is called 'syndication'. It's simply a method of selling the same thing over and over again. It is possible because many newspapers have clearly defined and limited circulation areas. So editor A in Blankshire won't be at all worried if you have sold the article he's buying to editor B in Pottle Wickley, because nobody in the Blankshire circulation area would see newspapers published in Pottle Wickley. For the same reason editor B won't be annoyed at publication in distant Blankshire, even if he ever gets to hear about it. If a Blankshire reader, by merest chance visiting relations in Pottle Wickley, reads what he already read in last week's paper at home, he will only feel a slight superiority that his home paper 'got there first', and no harm is done to either title.

All the same, if an article is being syndicated, i.e. has already been sold at least once elsewhere, you should indicate that this is so to any editor you offer it to. The fact that it has already met with approval somewhere else is likely to commend it to him: it's of proven marketable quality. He also knows it won't cost him as much as would non-syndicated copy, since you expect to be paid for it several times.

In this type of marketing a query letter is virtually essential. Use it to introduce yourself (briefly) and your wares (more fully) to newspaper editors in widely differing parts of the country. Freesheets buy a huge amount of syndicated material. It's a good idea to consult a marketing guide such as the *Writers' & Artists' Yearbook* (see Chapter 6) to study where newspaper groups may mean circulation areas overlap; purchase by a group may involve passing your copy to several titles within the group. Who would guess, for example, that papers in Portsmouth and Sunderland are under the same umbrella?

Because the fee for individual sales will be modest, it is not cost-effective to try syndicating work that doesn't have a better-than-average chance of being accepted. Maybe it's the comparatively humble reward that has given syndication a poor image. But weigh up the advantages: each payment is only part of what the copy may earn in its lifetime, there is no extra research or writing to be done, and your expense with each submission is small. Photocopying the copy and a short covering letter to recipients have been the only 'work'; envelopes and postage the total cost. You could call syndication money for jam. It is particularly easy if you have a large stock of useful copy (despatch a dozen or more items together for maximum impact and minimum trouble) and don't mind the jam being rather thinly spread on each piece.

There is another factor to consider, and that is the value you place on your time. The chores referred to above are a long way from writing. If I can't find anyone else to do them for me I combine most mechanical 'office' operations with taping potential research material or listening to a playback of interview notes. That way, stuffing paper into envelopes and sticking on stamps doesn't feel so boring. To my mind, syndication is only worthwhile if it can be accomplished as well as other useful work, not instead of it.

You might prefer to let someone else do the work of syndication for you. There are many agencies and some only take freelance copy. Of course they don't work for nothing and usual terms are a 50/50 split on all sales. In all cases do your market research of the agencies first. Write and ask what the agency is looking for; do they take freelance work? what style do they prefer? of what length? do they sell overseas? do they want only previously unpublished work? what are their rates? See the marketing guides referred to in Chapter 6 for details of some of these agencies.

The leading agencies are highly commercialised enterprises. Some state they're looking for professional writers with 'international minds', and most operate on a basic 15% handling charge. This means they send lists of ideas provided by their contributors (you?) to editors. The paper might then take up several ideas and want further details. All this will take place before any article is completed and the agency (taking its share of any fee going) might first pass your copy onto another agency. At this level it's big business and so are the slices taken from the rewards. At the flick of a keyboard what started as a £250 fee can shrink by 50% of 50% less deductions for this and that – and reach you as just £20. Hmm.

8
Business

P G Wodehouse didn't agree with Dr Johnson's dictum about only ever writing for money – and he was certainly no blockhead. 'I should think it extremely improbable,' he said, 'that anyone ever wrote anything simply for money. What makes a writer write is that he likes writing. Naturally, when he has written something, he wants to get as much for it as he can, but that is a very different thing from writing for money.

Some folk think that having a businesslike attitude sullies the art of writing. 'I'm a writer,' they claim, 'not a record-keeper.' The truth is that if you mean business you have to be both. Because I too want to be a writer and not a record-keeper I long ago devised a system that a) demands little time, b) keeps my affairs in order, and c) satisfies the Inland Revenue. That is why I urge you to study this chapter closely; not necessarily to model your own system on mine, but to appreciate the value of getting the 'business' straight from the beginning. You won't regret it.

Your status

A vital question to resolve the very day you decide to start writing is whether you are just a casual writer who indulges in it for a hobby or whether you are, or are soon going to be, a professional writer. Don't misunderstand that word 'professional'; you can be just as professional when you only write a couple of articles a year as when you are filing copy every day to a top national newspaper. Never think there is in any way a slur on being a dabbler. Countless writers want no other status and would certainly not wish to be caught up in what they see as a deal of paperwork and business hassle, especially if they have just retired from a lifetime of it. As for the quality of the finished product – the written word – that is what counts. The sun shines on us all without fear or favour, on some more, on others less; writing is to be enjoyed, and long may it be so.

I'm always embarrassed by any suggestion that a writer is someone 'precious' (especially if the suggestion is made by another writer) but having a purposeful self-image is not being arrogant. Being businesslike is itself good business. Working with your affairs and papers in a muddle will make life harder because you may not be able to find essential letters, agreements, blacks and other references when you want them, with the resultant mistakes and missed opportunities such confusion may generate. It will also give other people the impression that you are not likely to do a good job of work with your writing when you're in a state of constant chaos. Getting straight in your mind as well as on your desk is not just a matter of personal satisfaction (although if you truly are a professional freelance writer you will find yourself more confident and able to deal with many working situations more capably) but one of practical importance.

You and the Inland Revenue

If you happily class yourself as an occasional dabbler in the writing world you are likely to be assessed under Case VI of Schedule D of the Income and Corporation Taxes Act 1988, paying tax on the income from your dabblings and not being entitled to offset any expenses against tax. You may try to argue that your spasmodic writings are producing profits in what is a continuing business but this is plainly a self-contradiction few tax inspectors will accept, regarding you as either being in business or not being in business. You can't have it both ways, in the eyes of the Inland Revenue. Having said that I confess I personally know a few writers who *do* have it both ways; they earn very little, claim reasonable and wholly justifiable expenses to set against their earnings and end up with either a miniscule profit over the year, or even a loss. Writers are unique, they point out, and to them success is the personal satisfaction of writing, not sordid profit.

Bona fide freelance writers generally pay tax once a year directly to their tax offices. Give yourself this status and you can claim many benefits, setting some of your expenses against tax and even working at a tax loss. Of even greater value is being able, in most circumstances, to set any writing loss against your income from other sources. (The introduction of independent taxation in 1990 closed the loophole whereby you could prior to this date even set any loss against a spouse's income in the same financial year.)

To satisfy the Inland Revenue you must demonstrate that you are a professional writer, that you are trying to make a profit and that you are eligible to be taxed under Case II of Schedule D. This means your taxable income from writing will be the amount you receive in fees less expenses wholly and exclusively incurred in the pursuit of your writing. The taxman is not a big bad dragon when it comes to assessing freelance writers with small incomes, or even with no income, but he must be satisfied that you are working as a writer (researching, gathering material or engaged upon legitimate business, if not actually covering paper with words) with every serious intention of achieving publication. As a further demonstration of the Inland Revenue's sensible outlook (in this respect, if not in others) from April 1990 detailed tax accounts are no longer needed from small businesses. Taxpayers must still keep accurate records, but three line accounts are acceptable with tax returns.

If you hold another full-time job besides writing it may not be so easy to substantiate your writing credentials, but being able to produce genuine records and receipts, and to demonstrate a proper businesslike approach to your writing work will help. Sales, particularly regular ones, undoubtedly have the most impressive effect. A well-known writer whose novels are now bestsellers all over the world tells me he is still grateful to the Inland Revenue for the gentle treatment he received at the beginning of his career, even though – as he adds ruefully – 'I sometimes feel these days I'm being made to pay off the National Debt single-handed.'

When you earn money for your work, be it ever so little, the Inland Revenue will want to know. It's a mistake to think, 'A few pounds for fillers and some small cheques for articles I sold to X newspaper – that isn't worth bothering about.' Oh yes it is. Not only because there might be some awkward questions from the tax inspector when you become better known (not *if*, please note!) but because of those expenses you can set against any tax you might have to pay on your earnings.

Postage, stationery, telephone calls, printing headed paper and business cards, insurance (if taken out specially) and maintenance of equipment such as your typewriter or word-processor, tapes, disks, books of reference (including this one), travelling expenses, hotels, meals eaten out in the course of work, secretarial expenses, professional subscriptions, typewriter ribbons; once you start noting your expenses you'll be amazed how they add up. You may also amortize the original cost of whatever equipment you need, a typewriter, word-processor, cassette-recorder or any other major purchase, by claiming 20% or perhaps 25% (usually subject to the capital cost and by negotiation with the tax inspector) of the price paid in the first year, another 10% or 25% of the rest the following year – and so on, until the whole sum has been defrayed.

This may be a good spot to remind you that keeping your capital expenses in proportion to your anticipated income is only sensible, particularly at the beginning; and don't forget that your working time also counts as an expense.

In round figures I estimate a good idea has earned me 20% of the fee I eventually receive; this is quite a high proportion of the whole because experience has taught me the value of ideas *given other prerequisites*. Researching I count as worth a further 30% and writing it up another 40%. A section of this book is devoted to research, while a whole chapter expands on HOW TO WRITE IT. Is that 40% too low, then? Is not how-to-write what it's all about? Of course, but I can with some confidence assume you wouldn't have stayed with me – or indeed ever started this book – without at least some ability. You may be still trying your wings, you may have a good deal of published work behind you or you may fall somewhere between these levels but if you *really* want to succeed as a writer you *will* – of that I have no doubt. In a lifetime of writing I have got to know many hundreds, perhaps thousands, of writers and I've never met one who was not an optimist; privately, very often, and sometimes without admitting to it or being aware of it, but that quiet unshakeable optimism is the deepest support at the back of the mind when success seems far away. Writing is an easily abandoned occupation and to make the grade takes determination and staying power. Somewhere buried among those characteristics is the most important of all – an involuntary compulsion. Nobody forces you to do it as there are countless other ways of keeping the bills at bay, but a compulsion to write means you must. I count it a fortunate handicap (if it may even be called so) for writing is also a way of making money. It sound too good to be true, doesn't it? Especially to those who've never tried it.

Lastly comes my assessment of the selling of a piece of work and I consider that earns the final 10%. Again not enough, you think? With a new market or one I'm less familiar with I might adjust that percentage a little. But if I'm selling to a paper I've carefully reconnoitred or one to which I've already sold other stories, 10% is ample as there will be minimum effort involved in selling again.

Back to practicalities. Working out your hourly rate of pay after, say, the first six months can be a humbling experience, for by this I mean your hourly rate of pay on the whole job. My records at the end of each working day remind me of the proportion of time given to each activity; in this way I can decide to spend my time more profitably, or whether I wish to indulge myself with a specific project in future, knowing it will not be one that pays for itself, let alone makes a profit.

Keep whatever receipts, invitations, details of meetings, travel tickets and even diaries that come your way to produce for the taxman if he wants to see them; it's improbable that he will, but you never know. Everything that serves to demonstrate your status as an established freelance is worth saving. Are you attending a writers' conference or school to further your knowledge and experience? Claim those fees, of course – and the cost of getting there and back.

It may be hard to work out exactly how much your car costs you when you are wearing your freelance writer's hat, unless you reserve the car for that purpose alone, which is hardly likely to be the case. Mileage allowances vary greatly, the current rates being as low as 15 pence a mile and the highest about 40 pence; you may have heard of a higher figure being paid. A written confirmation of the rate customarily granted to journalists on the staff of any paper you write for regularly may encourage the taxman to allow you the same rate. Otherwise you should put in a claim at a 'reasonable' rate – see the NUJ and Society of Author's guides. It may be even harder to convince the Inland Revenue when you come to claiming for car maintenance and depreciation as these vary even more depending on the model, age and mileage of your car.

Do you work in a room in your house specially set aside for the purpose? Notwithstanding 1990 changes in the rating system (1989 in Scotland) you may legitimately claim for the light, heating and cleaning of your work room, plus whatever proportion of rent (if any) it represents in relation to what you pay. In the days of the old rating system it was also possible to claim rates relief for your writing space in proportion to what you paid for the whole house. But since the Community Charge is a tax on individuals and not a tax on property this relief is no longer allowed. You should also be aware that although exemption from Capital Gains Tax applies to your house (or your main house if you own more than one) it does *not* apply to whatever part of it you use for carrying on a business. This means that if and when you sell the house you will have to pay Capital Gains Tax on that portion of it deemed to be appropriate to the whole. This penalty only applies to *exclusive* use of a room (or rooms) for your work and tax is payable at your highest income rate – currently 25% for basic rate taxpayers and 40% for higher rate payers. It is quite legitimate to claim that the room where you write is *not* exclusively a work room if you use it for domestic purposes as well – even if only occasionally. Anyone is free to work from home, but you may need planning permission if you want to build a special extension as a workplace. If you have a mortgage you should tell your lender what you plan to do, if your home is rented check with your landlord first, and if you live in council premises let the housing officer know.

Furthermore, you will be able to claim expenses incurred before you actually earn anything at all, providing you tell the Inland Revenue from the beginning that you are in business as a writer. Your work may, for instance, take three or four years to research before a word of the finished product is written, and you may carry forward a sum covering 'work in progress' for many years, although this is more likely to be the working pattern of book writers than journalists, particularly newspaper journalists. But for all, good record-keeping is wise. With it, in theory, you needn't fear the shadow of the Inland Revenue, while also being fair to your own pocket.

Why only 'in theory'? To the dismay of professional freelances working casual or occasional shifts in newspaper offices (as many do), by the end of 1989 all national and an increasing number of provincial papers had been instructed by the Inland Revenue to deduct from fees paid to freelances income tax (ignoring personal allowances) and national insurance contributions. You can guess that such a period of work can play havoc with your tax position; getting back the excess tax you have paid during a few weeks working in an office rather than in your own home can take months or even years. I speak from ghastly and unforgettable personal experience. Many magazine publishers are now doing the same (the system was introduced into IPC in April 1990) and it seems inevitable that this practice will eventually extend to freelances working outside offices as well. There has been no new legislation; merely a new interpretation of existing law.

Confusingly, while the Inland Revenue may cast us down, the Treasury offers more comfort. The former states 'there is no statutory definition of employment or self-employment' and 'the term *freelance* does not mean self-employed'; the latter 'there is certainly no question of the Revenue insisting that tax is deducted by companies from payments made to those who are genuinely self-employed'. The London freelance branch of the National Union of Journalists (see Chapter 6) is investigating this fearsome development and organising opposition to it. A great deal may rest on the outcome for all freelance writers, including those who have never worked in a newspaper office and don't wish to do so.

It will certainly help to behave at all times as a self-employed writer rather than as an employee. Use private headed stationery and work on your own equipment. Make sure you are paid on the basis of work done, not hours worked. Make your own arrangements for insurance, pensions and so on, and (probably the best safeguard against taxation at source) do not work exclusively for one market. It is hard to convince the Inland Revenue of your freelance status unless you work, or have worked, for at least three or four different employers in the course of a single tax year.

Many NUJ freelances move from office to office working alongside staffers, but getting no staff benefits, holidays, sick pay, maternity or parental leave, service increments, employer-paid training or even normal expenses. The advantages of their *freelance* tax status makes the work worthwhile, even with such disadvantages. (Incidentally, be wary about accepting staff privileges when you do a small regular task, as this may affect your freelance status.)

Writers (like everyone else in the same boat) with incomes from writing currently greater than £25,400 per year or £8,600 in one quarter must register as payers of Value Added Tax with HM Customs & Excise. Those earning less than these figures may also register, at the discretion of HM Customs & Excise, and may obtain certain benefits thereby.

Keeping records

So when you adopt professional status you will be either a writer who is a full-time freelance with a steady stream of work accepted and paid for during the year, a 'hobby' scribbler with a different full-time job, perhaps, just turning winter evenings into success in a handful of publications, or somewhere in the varieties of writing that lie between the two. Whichever category of freelance writing you fall into, taking trouble with record-keeping now, as you go along, will save you a great deal more later.

The best method is simple to use and understand. In all aspects of writing it's a mistake to let the tail wag the dog by setting up a method you can't instantly recall when you pick it up after being away. A hard-backed book with lined pages is ideal as an 'expenses book'. Rule a few columns as you wish, and make it a habit to log whatever you spend every day, every mile you travel, every phone call you make and every stamp you lick. (Actually this last can be a pain; I buy sheets of stamps to be used solely for business mail and keep them in a special pigeon-hole at my desk, so they don't get confused with other stamps used for domestic and private letters.) I've always found it easy to record my entries only on the right-hand pages of an Expenses Book; the book naturally falls open with the right-hand page facing me waiting to be written on, and such is the usage it gets that it usually presents itself to me on the current page. I paper-clip receipts relevant to each page onto the left-hand pages.

Just as simple is a system of keeping track of manuscripts, where I send them, when and what their fate is. My manuscript (ms) book is also lined but I prefer to have no columns, apart from one for the date at the beginning of the line. Each piece of work I do, be it long or short (including Letters to the Editor), is given a number which is written in red at the top right corner of a new right-hand page or the portion of a page devoted to a new piece of work. This number, incidentally, also identifies it immediately when in due course it is pasted in one of my archive albums – see the final chapter 'And Afterwards' . . .). The title and length of the work is centred below with the date on which it was despatched and its destination on the line below that. Then follows a space awaiting news of its date of publication and the fee paid with its date. Now here's the rub: I know a commissioned piece of work will be sold without any fuss (or I've gone horribly wrong somewhere) so it will only need a few blank lines on which to record its history. I can leave a little space for forthcoming details, rule a line across the page and start recording the next piece of work below it. Only when I am not sure how long it may be before a piece is accepted, published and paid for will I leave plenty of space for its history – and I don't like copy with a long history. To the left page opposite the work I paper-clip correspondence, agreements, payment letters and any other relevant pieces of paper. Pages at the back of the book also record which papers have bought my copy, when and their rates at the time. On disk (this snippet of information is for computer-owning writers only) I also keep an instantly accessible spreadsheet showing me full details of all the above at the touch of a key. Like many writers I'm in love with my word-processor and cannot now imagine writing anything without it. The ease with which the computer also deals with accounts, keeping records and presenting me with instant assistance in all aspects of the business side of a writer's life is marvellous to behold...and the subject of books other than this one.

S

Getting advice and help

At the beginning of your writing career you may feel it is littered with traps and perils for the innocent; you have no desire to defraud the Inland Revenue and are frightened of unwittingly doing so. Take heart. If your bank manager or friendly solicitor is helpful but lacks the particular expertise required in this field, the Small Firms Service run by the Department of Trade and Industry will supply you with a free pack of business information specially for the self-employed. The Citizen's Advice Bureau may also help and although its staff may not be quite specialised enough for your circumstances, they and other community enterprises offer free advice and will at least tell you where to find more. See also Chapter 6, 'Help and Where to Find It'.

Because writers without any other job or profession are self-employed and 'on their own' you might need to think of taking out a private pension, planning your tax distribution over the years, or making personal insurance provision. You'll soon find that dealing with all this is a considerable intrusion on your writing time; in these matters, and in others, an accountant wtih specialised knowledge and experience in this field will be invaluable – and you can, of course, set his charges against tax.

Rights to offer and to keep

When you are employed by a newspaper, i.e. you are a full-time or part-time staff member, the copyright of everything you write for that paper is owned by its proprietor. A confusing fact is that a separate copyright exists as soon as a piece is published, and it is this that newspapers create when they print copy written by members of their staff – who are, by the nature of their contracts, barred (except in very special circumstances) from selling their 'original' copyright elsewhere. A similar restraint assigns the copyright of business writers and teachers to companies and education authorities etc., if their work is written in the course of employment by such bodies. The copyright sign of © designed by the Universal Copyright Convention is not required by law in the UK but is the only way to ensure protection in countries such as the USA and Russia which are (like us) members of the Convention but are not also members of the Berne Convention as we are.

But if you are writing as a freelance contributor the copyright of what you have written remains in your hands (except in circumstances so rare we may almost forget about them) and when you offer your work to a paper you are merely offering the first British serial rights, i.e. your permission for the paper to be the first to print and publish your copy in this country. This being well-understood and taken to be so by default, it is neither customary nor necessary to write 'First British Serial Rights' on copy sent to newspapers. It is also an understood part of the deal that a newspaper, which may be published in several editions at the same time, has the right to use work accepted from freelances in more than one edition, this being, in effect, 'one' usage only.

So what about this 'separate' copyright the paper owns once it has bought your work? While the literal contents of the written piece remain with the author it is this separate copyright covering its exact typographical layout that is now owned by the newspaper. Is it, then, free to use it again later or sell it to someone else? In theory, yes, *in the exact typographical layout in which it first appeared*. But what paper likes to use the same copy twice? 'I've read this before,' cynical readers would snort. 'Are they short of something to print?' As for rivals – would any want to print someone else's old copy? You think the paper you sold to might change the layout and try to sell your work overseas? It's possible they might, and if they did they would be stealing the contents and infringing your copyright. There just may be a handful who'd think it worth having a go if the subject matter were of great importance, but if it were of enough intrinsic value for them to sell again, you would be able to do so yourself first.

Knowing the established rules and practice about copyright should set minds at rest, but it cannot, alas, be claimed that all papers stick strictly to them. Indeed one or two newspaper groups make no secret of assuming you are giving them all rights. With a few a particularly cunning trick you may come across is finding an endorsement on the back of your cheque glibly assigning the paper everything, i.e. depriving you of all rights. You might be facing this ominous (and illegal) statement on the cheque requiring that you should sign agreement perhaps weeks or even months after the piece has been bought and published – so what do you do? Some ultra-cautious folk return the cheque to the paper, asking for it to be amended; they might receive an apology for the 'error', or they might hear nothing and not even get the cheque back without a battle. In fact no such correspondence is needed, for the answer is simple: cross through the claim firmly and present the cheque to the bank as usual. If there is any trouble about it from the paper in future, which is unlikely, you may have to remind them they are acting illegally and cannot take what you have not offered, any more than I can take the whole cake if you only offer me a slice. Still nervous? Be reassured by the fact that most writers happily published in newspapers all their writing lives never encounter this difficulty at all.

Some worrying news thumped through the letterboxes of all NUJ freelances towards the end of 1989 when details began to emerge about a new interpretation of the Copyright Act. It appeared that some publishers of both large and smaller circulation papers (and magazines) have been trying to persuade freelance writers into giving up all rights for no extra pay, with the hint that if they didn't agree they might find their work less readily acceptable in future. Although the law confers various rights on writers we may, of course, waive those rights if we wish or are persuaded to do so. My advice to such a suggestion or request from a publisher, should you receive one, is 'don't sign away all rights'; both principle and practice are at risk of being compromised.

A similar danger exists in contracts sometimes offered to freelances. Many moons ago (when I began working for *The Sun*) a contract was confirmation of intent to serve by one side and security of employment by the other. Clauses dealt with the matter of rights, among other things, agreeing to the normal provisions then obtaining; the writer retained the copyright, licensing it to the paper (a daily) to be released after a period of fourteen days. In my case this meant I handed over copyright of everything I wrote for the paper for just a fortnight, after which it reverted to me to use elsewhere and in whatever manner I wished. (I may say that a daily column accumulates an enormous amount of copy over a long period and I have, with the copyright in my sole hands, been able to make extensive and profitable use of it ever since.)

Agreeable as writers are when you meet them at seminars and conferences (few groups of potential rivals are so friendly and willing to share their trade secrets) it is naïve to imagine there aren't a few baddies seeking the easy way into their ranks. Those who lack the ability to write for themselves are not above stealing what is already written by other people. You need to be ever watchful that yours is not the material stolen by an idle so-called writer who hopes neither you nor anyone else will notice the theft.

But the copying machine is a two-edged piece of modern equipment and you must also be careful that in researching for what you want to write you don't unthinkingly infringe the copyright of those whose work you're consulting. What is considered 'fair dealing' is confined by a thin line unwittingly crossed by the unwary. It is fair to make a single copy of someone else's work for purposes of private study and this may extend to copying a couple of pages from a reference book. Copying a large section means trouble. But the definition of 'large' in this context remains unclear.

Imagine you are reporting a speech made by a leading public figure and need to quote his exact words in your newspaper report. Written drafts of many such speeches are handed round to the waiting press before they're delivered on a platform. You are quite free to reproduce his exact words as he says them, but what if you also (then or on another occasion) copy his words from the press handout? By common consent this is allowable as long as your quote from the written speech copies it only to a reasonable extent. Again, what is reasonable? How long is a piece of string? Nobody can tell you the precise answer, but I keep my pieces of string short enough to be entirely safe. It's easy to do this; there are a dozen ways of breaking up potentially dangerous quotes or passages (see Chaper 4, 'How to Write It'). In fact if you're reporting the words of politicians and others used to the sound of their own voices in public, you may well be doing the rest of us a service by lightening the text, without losing any of its meaning.

A final word on this topic: copyright lies in the expression of ideas, not in the ideas themselves. But don't spread your best ideas about too liberally. Other people may flood the market with their interpretations of your ideas before you get round to writing about them yourself – and when you do you may find the freshness has gone.

What should you be paid?

The matter of 'rates of pay' should be at the front of your mind when you are thinking about aspects of setting yourself up in business. 'How much will I be paid?' is a question, perhaps more than any other, so tangled and giving rise to so wide a range of opinions that few freelances can agree on the answer, while many deny there can be one.

In my experience such imprecision is just what editors like and as long as it persists they see no reasons for clarifying the position. Put yourself in their shoes; most are no stingier than the rest of us, but the less it costs to run their papers the greater favour they're likely to find from their owners or proprietors. Naturally they don't want to be expected, let alone forced, to pay more than the low rates some can get away with now.

It's sad to hear of freelance writers so pleased to have their work accepted at all that they'll gratefully accept whatever fee is offered; some don't even know what they're going to be given until they receive it or some document reveals how much it's going to be. Can you imagine a worker in any other occupation being content with such a loose and unsatisfactory arrangement? Do you believe the newsprint suppliers, the van drivers, the secretarial staff and all the other people employed in the running of a newspaper don't know their rates of pay? Would managements or editors dream of treating them as so many of them treat freelances? Regular staff writers, please note, have a structured and recognised scale of salaries; they wouldn't put up with the treatment frequently meted out to freelances. The labour force essential to make a newspaper work depends on writers as much as it does on other workers in the industry. Managements must, of course, secure the services of staff journalists by paying them at a regular and mutually agreed rate. Freelances are lower down the scale, you say, and therefore can't expect to be treated as decently? Well, if you're resigned to being thought of as a second-class writer and don't mind being trampled on....

The usual (and some claim unalterable) method of paying freelance writers is virtually unknown in any other sphere. Shall I accept a coat, for instance, that a local market stallholder proffers, take it home without paying for it, hang it up in the wardrobe for a few weeks, months or even years – and then casually mention to the stallholder that I don't want it and he can have it back? Pity it's got a bit dirty and crumpled since falling on the floor and a couple of buttons are missing, but that doesn't matter, does it? Shall I try doing that and see what happens? It's not the same? I can't see the difference. When I offer a piece of work to an editor (commission apart), I am like the stallholder offering that coat. The potential purchaser either wants it and is prepared to pay for it, or doesn't want it and hands it back immediately. Why should it be acceptable for an editor, a potential purchaser of manuscripts, to behave in so cavalier a fashion? The question of how-much-I-should be paid for an accepted piece of work and when-it-should-be-paid are dealt with elsewhere but in dealing with this sometimes thorny topic I do urge writers not to sell their work for a pittance.

I realise some may be writing as freelances in their retirement, as an extra interest while fully employed in another job, or because they enjoy writing but really do not need the money (and of course there is nothing wrong with any of those circumstances in themselves). However, the 'I'm not bothered about the fees' brigade don't understand how much harder they are making life for their fellow writers, and even for themselves. Amateurs are fine. I was one once and so was every other writer. But editors know *perpetual* amateurs don't expect much – and that is why they don't get it.

Many freelances are writing full-time with mouths to feed and mortgages to pay but publishers and newspaper proprietors aren't worried about whether they need the money or not. Life can be tough. As long as editors (or whoever fixes rates of pay) can find writers willing to work for little or nothing, they'll know that's all they need offer. Perhaps the hardest lesson for beginning writers to learn (and, I regret to say, some of those willing to take 'anything' in the cause of getting published are not still beginners) is **Do Not Undercut Your Worth or Your Colleagues by Accepting Less than Professional Fees**. 'But if I ask for more they won't buy my work!' you may be protesting. Have you been firm

enough to try? Tell a meanie editor you think his offer is too
low and you expect £X for the job – and see what happens. If
he rejects you at least you will know whom to avoid in future.
But provided you have shown him you can offer thoroughly
professional copy that he really wants, when he wants it, he
won't turn you away. And afterwards he'll not only respect
you but know you can be relied on to do another good job next
time. The world can be hard and freelance writing is not easy;
be a wimp and you'll be treated like one; be competent and
diligent and you'll find plenty of work at fair rates.

NUJ rates of pay

It is a surprise to many freelances to learn there is an official
list of what is considered 'fair' payment by various
newspapers and magazines. The National Union of
Journalists issue their freelance members (there are more than
6,000 of them) with an annual Guide, from which the
following are extracts. I stress that all the figures quoted are
basic rates from which negotiation should start:

National daily newspapers
Features: £175 per 1000 words
Reviews: £135 per 1000 words
Home news: £16.20 per 200 words or part thereof
Foreign, city & business news: £16.50 per 100 words

Sunday papers
Features: £200 per 1000 words
Reviews: £150 per 1000 words
Special rates for front or back lead story: from £325
Crosswords: £65 to £75; diary paragraphs: £35 to £80;
supplements (seldom other than by commission): from £225
per 1000 words

All the above rates apply to *The Independent*, *The Guardian*, *The
Observer*, the *Glasgow Herald*, the *Daily Record*, the *Scotsman*,
Scotland on Sunday and the *Manchester Evening News*.

Provincial papers
Dailies
Up to and including 10 lines: £1.95 per line (*per single column
width*) with 15p each additional line

Features on spec: up to and including 10 lines: £2.14 per line, additionals 16p
Features commissioned: £143

Weeklies
Up to and including 10 lines: £1.10 per line with 11p each additional line
Features on spec: up to and including 10 lines: £1.22 per line, additionals 12p
Features commissioned: £102

Regional and evenings
Features commissioned: £117

If you feel your head is in cloud cuckoo land (or, more probably, that mine is) after reading the figures above, remember those 6,000 NUJ freelances who earn their livelihood by doing nothing else but writing. Could they, as well as non-NUJ freelances in great numbers, survive from writing alone if there were not a properly negotiated structure of payment? It is true that not every paper, high and low, subscribes to these agreed rates, but the majority do, with the smaller ones usually belonging to greater parent groups who do. I stress that poor quality work cannot expect to receive much reward, for it is probably not worth much, but next time you're offered derisory rates for a *first-class job*, ask yourself who's kidding whom?

Whatever you think you ought to be paid, or would like to receive, don't forget to update your ideas every year in line with inflation; the rates a paper paid you a couple of years ago, or even last year, should not be what they are paying now. 'Rates of pay' are usually defined in terms of the number of words written (caution: the paper may interpret this as payment for words published, which may not be the same) but should you have specialist journalistic skills and be offered temporary work in a newspaper office it will be necessary to negotiate in terms of hours worked and an hourly rate. These can also be found in the NUJ Guide referred to above.

Plagiarism

The infringement of copyright, whether others do it to yours or you do it to theirs and regardless of whether it is deliberate or innocent, is called plagiarism. The history of literature is riddled with it, from the time an ancient Egyptian scribe found temporary fame by 'lifting' the words an earlier sage had written on the sides of a pillaged tomb, to the alleged plagiarism of a well-known Roald Dahl story and parts of Margaret Mitchell's *Gone with the Wind*. (Lawyers and in-born newspapermen/women among you may notice how instinctively the word 'alleged' stuck itself in there; omitting that important adjective, and thereby implying an accused is guilty before it has been proved so, has caused many a writer and newspaper horrible trouble.)

In cases where big-selling works are said to have been victims of plagiarism (there goes that caution again; habit will out) huge sums of money may be awarded in compensation if they are proved, but in smaller cases which some folk may think hardly worth bothering about the principle remains. Plagiarism is theft, and there's no refuting that.

Non-fiction work is particularly dangerous in this respect; researching a topic will often take different researchers down the same paths because they are the logical and reasonable paths to follow. How do you deal with raw facts and figures? Write that Josiah Blogsworth invented sandpaper in Harrogate in 1623 (I do hope he didn't because I think I've just invented him) and will you be guilty of plagiarism because a book you consulted in your research said he did? Hardly, any more than you could be in trouble for mentioning the earth is round and cats can't read. Plagiarism is a complex matter but it doesn't deal in nonsense. Like copyright, it needs to be studied and have its awesomeness appreciated before being stored (for all time, we hope) under the bed.

9
And Afterwards...

I went to insure my car a few months ago with a company new to me, being disillusioned with the one I'd used for years. In the offices of the new company a polite counter clerk handed me a quotation form and I began filling it in on the spot. He watched with a helpful smile until against the query 'occupation' I wrote 'journalist'. Abruptly his attitude changed and he reached across the counter to snatch the form away. 'We don't cover journalists,' he snapped. 'They drink too much, drive like maniacs and never tell the truth.'

Consider that verdict on this honourable calling. Although all three criticisms may, with justification, be levelled at a few of us some of the time, that last charge is hard to bear, drinkers, drivers, or neither. Journalists have a poor image. What can we do – what can *you* do – to improve our reputation?

I believe being in a position to write about other people imposes on us a moral responsibility to tell the truth as it appears to us. That means not only in news reports or when dealing with facts and figures, but also in the way we represent people, their circumstances and their lives. We must never belittle them or write anything to make them look foolish or less worthy than we find them. Just as speech may be given variety of meaning with accompanying raised eyebrows or a mock-severity, so what we write may be carelessly (or, alas, deliberately) laden with innuendo: the journalistic sneer, the glib approach, the suave assertions made over innocent people's heads. Such insinuation cheapens journalism because it is writing with less than honesty – and it's disgraceful. If we want the public to trust us we must first show ourselves to be trustworthy.

The benefits of success – and rejection

When you reach the stage of knowing what you're doing in

this business of writing for newspapers, 'what to write', 'how to write it' and 'where to sell it' will be your instinctive reactions to everything going on around you. As a freelance you'll realise success is a journey and not a destination, for everything you've learned and will continue to learn emphasises that professional integrity is what counts; and to that I'd add *calmness*. So it is a curious paradox that the results of success can be difficult to bear.

Newspaper journalists are ready to take knocks and very soon become used to them. For no matter how much you try not to upset anyone or what pains you have taken not to offend any of your likely readers, it is inevitable that one day someone somewhere will take exception to something you've written. What's to be done? Your first thought might be to get an apology printed to get yourself out of trouble. This is easier said than done for it may seem as if the people you hoped would be 'on your side' are the very ones to scupper your chances. No paper wants to print an acknowledgement that it made a mistake in an earlier edition. Getting one to print an apology or retraction may be impossible, except under legal pressure – and then you can be sure the amendment will be as small and insignificantly placed as possible.

A line has been omitted from your copy, or two lines have been transposed, making nonsense of one of the sentences that gave you most satisfaction? Your scrupulous punctuation has gone to pot with an outbreak of unwanted apostrophes, a couple of pars have been inverted and the final line rounding your copy off so neatly is missing altogether? What aggravation – and what should you do about it? You'd be foolish to go storming off to the editor, or to any of his underlings.

Like every journalist I've had my share of irritations – and I expect there are more in the pipeline for me just waiting for stories I haven't yet written. Pray they won't all cause such chaos as happened after a thoughtless sub-editor omitted from my recipe for home-made ginger beer (in a national daily) the essential line about using *corks* and not screwtops to allow the fermentation an escape route. The paper's switchboard was jammed with protests about my dangerous ignorance and an exploding bottle blew a hole in a bungalow's roof in Colwyn Bay. Before someone was injured or any further damage was done, the paper was forced to print a correction, a large one in a prominent position. It didn't like doing so, and for quite a while I wasn't popular. As for the sub-editor who caused all the trouble – well, nobody gave him a thought. And I realised the sooner I forgot any grievance I felt justified in harbouring, the better for us all.

When something like this happens a deep breath and a private sigh at the inefficiencies of everyone but you are all you may allow yourself. Just watch lest the next mistake is yours, for without constant alertness we all succumb to complacency and carelessness. Only recently someone pointed out to me that the small town of Altrincham is spelt with a 'c' in the middle. It is a place I've often need to refer to and I had for *years* been spelling it 'Altringham'.

Despite all our hopes for success it could be that failure and rejection make better writers in the long run. Meeting the challenge of continual disappointment with a strong determination to succeed will certainly prove any writer's ability. But stubborn persistence is not enough; banging your head against a brick wall will – eventually – only wear down your head. Finding another way of breaking down the wall is the solution; failure, after all, is only an opportunity to do it again – better. That's the professional way. And it's amazing that the more professional you are, the more editors need you.

Yesterday's story

Time, for a busy newspaper journalist, has the not unpleasant habit of piling up copy. Soon the papers carrying what you've written can fill your shelves, lie in untidy heaps on the floor and be stacked in piles up the stairs. One day you'll get round to cutting out your work and putting it away safely. Where? And how?

Tear-sheets (cuttings of your columns, features, news stories or whatever you want to keep) may be very conveniently stored in albums. I acquire the large hard-covered ones commercial printers use to show their potential customers Christmas cards and other lines. If you would like to do the same find such a printer (there's bound to be at least one in every town) and ask if he will give you several of these albums when he's finished with them – which will generally be in the early part of the year. Most printers will readily agree, especially if you have tactfully used their services yourself (not necessarily in the Christmas card line) as they only throw these albums away when their display of current cards is out of date. I have dozens of such albums for my archives and find they serve the purpose ideally. They are easy to label, printed tear-sheets show up well on their pages, and their sturdiness retards newsprint from yellowing with age.

Agreeable as it may be to browse through your archive material, with its attendant glow of recollection, archives are not just for providing you with a nostalgic boost. They can give more valuable service when you view them as your very own research material for future work. Old copy can be useful, updated in the light of more recent events. With other research that led you to write about the topic months or years ago (you do keep research material, don't you?) you may find an original viewpoint not covered by those confining themselves to up-to-date investigations. And it's surprising how often stories crop up again long after their original topicality or popularity. It seems even we journalists, so frequently castigated by the general public, have a phoenix occasionally smiling on us.

And tomorrow's

Who can see into the future? Are those folk who predicted the demise of printed newspapers years ago going to have the last laugh after all? Already, in some places, today's newspapers are put on teletext overnight for special categories of viewers (the physically handicapped, for example), and this morning's paper can be read on the screen in the afternoon. Is the death of the conventional newspaper inevitable?

However news might be printed and distributed, journalists are still going to be needed to write what is read. According to the eighteenth-century politician Edmund Burke, this *Fourth Estate* of ours is 'more important far than they all' (Thomas Carlyle: *Heroes and Hero-Worship*).

Be a freelance journalist and you shoulder a responsibility that will keep you on your toes. When the ink gets into your veins, there's no job to beat it.

And that, as they say, is the bottom line.

Index